**TRAVERSE
THEATRE**

SCOTLAND'S NEW WRITING THEATRE

Traverse Theatre Company in association with
the Royal Shakespeare Company

Fall

by Zinnie Harris

cast in order of appearance

Kate	Geraldine Alexander
Evener	Cliff Burnett
Guard	Brian Ferguson
Liddel	Kevin McMonagle
Pierre	Darrell D'Silva
Kiki	Meg Fraser
Howard	Paul Hickey
Justine	Samantha Young

Director	Dominic Hill
Designer	Tom Piper
Lighting Designer	Chahine Yavroyan
Sound Designer	Dan Jones

Stage Manager	Gemma Smith
Deputy Stage Manager	Alison Brodie
Assistant Stage Manager	Dan Dixon

**first performed at the Traverse Theatre,
Thursday 24 July 2008**

a Traverse Theatre Commission

THE TRAVERSE

Artistic Director Dominic Hill

A Rolls-Royce machine for promoting new Scottish drama across Europe and beyond.
(The Scotsman)

The Traverse's commissioning process embraces a spirit of innovation and risk-taking that has launched the careers of many of Scotland's best-known writers including John Byrne, David Greig, David Harrower and Liz Lochhead. It is unique in Scotland in that it fulfils the crucial role of providing the infrastructure, professional support and expertise to ensure the development of a dynamic theatre culture for Scotland.

The importance of the Traverse is difficult to overestimate . . . without the theatre, it is difficult to imagine Scottish playwriting at all. (Sunday Times)

From its conception in the 1960s, the Traverse has remained a pivotal venue in Edinburgh. It receives enormous critical and audience acclaim for its programming, as well as regularly winning awards. Most recently, Alan Wilkins' commission for the Traverse, *Carthage Must Be Destroyed*, won Best New Play at the 2008 Critics Awards for Theatre in Scotland. From 2001–07, Traverse productions of *Gagarin Way* by Gregory Burke, *Outlying Islands* by David Greig, *Iron* by Rona Munro, *The People Next Door* by Henry Adam, *Shimmer* by Linda McLean, *When the Bulbul Stopped Singing* by Raja Shehadeh, *East Coast Chicken Supper* by Martin J Taylor, *Strawberries in January* by Evelyne de la Chenelière in a version by Rona Munro and *Damascus* by David Greig have won Fringe First or Herald Angel awards (and occasionally both).

In 2007 the Traverse's Festival programme *Faithful* picked up an incredible 12 awards including Fringe Firsts for Tim Crouch's *ENGLAND* (a Traverse commission) and the Traverse Theatre production of *Damascus* by David Greig, plus a Herald Archangel for outgoing Artistic Director Philip Howard for "his consistent and lasting contribution to Edinburgh's Festivals".

The Traverse Theatre has established itself as Scotland's leading exponent of new writing, with a reputation that extends worldwide. (The Scotsman)

The Traverse's success isn't limited to the Edinburgh stage. Since 2001, Traverse productions of *Gagarin Way, Outlying Islands, Iron, The People Next Door, When the Bulbul Stopped Singing*, the *Slab Boys*

Trilogy, Mr Placebo and *Helmet* have toured not only within Scotland and the UK, but in Sweden, Norway, the Balkans, Germany, USA, Iran, Jordan and Canada. Immediately following the 2006 festival, the Traverse's production of *Petrol Jesus Nightmare #5 (In the Time of the Messiah)* by Henry Adam was invited to perform at the International Festival in Priština, Kosovo and won the Jury Special Award for Production. During spring 2008, the Traverse toured its award winning 2007 production of *Damascus* to Toronto, New York and Moscow.

One of Europe's most important homes for new plays.
(Sunday Herald)

The Traverse's work with young people is of supreme importance and takes the form of encouraging playwriting through its flagship education project *Class Act*, as well as the Young Writers' Group. *Class Act* is now in its 18th year and gives school pupils the opportunity to develop their plays with professional playwrights and work with directors and actors to see the finished piece performed on stage at the Traverse. This year, for the fourth year running, the project also took place in Russia. The hugely successful Young Writers' Group is open to new writers aged 18 - 25 with fortnightly meetings led by a professional playwright. In Autumn 2008 the Traverse will, for the first time, work with young men from HM Young Offenders Institution Polmont to improve their literacy skills through practical drama and playwriting. The participants will work with theatre professionals to develop their own plays which will be performed both at HM YOI Polmont and at the Traverse.

The Traverse has an unrivalled reputation for producing contemporary theatre of the highest quality, invention and energy, and for its dedication to new writing. (Scotland on Sunday)

The Traverse is committed to working with international playwrights and, in 2005, produced *In the Bag* by Wang Xiaoli in a version by Ronan O'Donnell, the first ever full production of a contemporary Chinese play in the UK. This project was part of the successful Playwrights in Partnership scheme, which unites international and Scottish writers, and brings the most dynamic new global voices to the Edinburgh stage. Other international Traverse partnerships have included work in Québec, Norway, Finland, France, Italy, Portugal and Japan.

www.traverse.co.uk

RSC New Writing

We are proud to be working in association with the Traverse on this production of Zinnie Harris' *Fall*. The play completes a trilogy which began with the RSC's production of *Midwinter* in 2005. Zinnie played a key part in invigorating the RSC's return to its roots as a new play producer. The first two parts of her trilogy were central to Dominic Cooke's New Work Festivals in 2005 and 2006. As our Stratford home is being redeveloped, we are delighted that Dominic Hill has been able to inspire and produce this wonderful final play in Zinnie's trilogy.

We wish Dominic the very best in his first Festival as Artistic Director and we are looking forward to this new relationship with the Traverse.

The RSC away from Stratford

Later this year we continue our renewed commitment to contemporary writers with new work by Adriano Shaplin and Marina Carr. Both plays will be produced in the faded decadence of Wilton's Music Hall in London. We are also continuing our commitment to touring Shakespeare, playing at venues around the UK, including Glasgow, Brighton and Cardiff. Last year, the RSC spent 47 weeks touring and playing residences in the UK and around the world, playing to almost 200,000 people in venues as far afield as Canada's National Arts Centre, Davidson College in North Carolina and the Singapore Repertory Theatre.

Shakespeare the writer

Shakespeare is our in-house playwright. Central to the work of the RSC is the opportunity to investigate his influence on modern writers. We focus equally on new work and classics and we believe that this duality gives us our dynamism. We believe that our Shakespearean productions need to embrace the vitality of the world we live in, and the best way to do this is to produce Shakespeare alongside contemporary plays full of new ideas and insights.

We will be producing more new plays over the coming seasons, and working with living writers in the Shakespeare rehearsal room. Looking at how writers' imaginations influence the process of making theatre will become part of the investigation into the classics. We hope and believe that this reconnection of living writers with our House Playwright will become one of the most exciting and mutually nourishing relationships in theatre. Shakespeare is a great teacher. He knows how to marry the recognisable with the lyrical, and the entertaining with the profound. There is a vast array of skills and stagecraft which we are inviting contemporary dramatists to plunder as they join the actors, directors, musicians and designers in wrestling Shakespeare's beauty and vigour onto our stages.

COMPANY BIOGRAPHIES

Geraldine Alexander (*Kate*)
Geraldine trained at RADA and the NYT, and began her career at Pitlochry Festival Theatre. Theatre credits include *I Saw Myself* (The Wrestling School); *The Maids* (Brighton Festival); *Titus Andronicus, A Midsummer Night's Dream, The Tempest, The Two Noble Kinsmen, The Maid's Tragedy* (Shakespeare's Globe); *Pillars of the Community* (Royal National Theatre); *Holy Terror* (West End); *The Seagull, A Woman of No Importance, Present Laughter, Hamlet* (Manchester Royal Exchange); *The Real Thing* (Bristol Old Vic/National Tour); *Inconceivable* (West Yorkshire Playhouse/National Tour); *A Streetcar Named Desire* (Colchester); *Flesh and Blood, Private Lives, Jude the Obscure* (Method & Madness); *Stargazey Pie & Saucraut* (Royal Court Theatre); *Twelfth Night, The Plain Dealer, Richard III, Hamlet* (Royal Shakespeare Company). Television & Film credits include *Silent Witness, Taggart, Extras, Feel the Force, Love Soup, Midsommer Murders, Coronation Street, The Government Inspector, Dance to the Music of Time, The Vacillations of Poppy Carew, Bomber, Forgotten, Bright Hair, Poirot, Miss Marple – Fatal Passage, Messages,* and *Mechant Garcon.* Radio credits include *Henry IV Parts 1 & 2, School for Scandal, Jumping the Rug, Easy Virtue, The Airman Who Would Not Die.*

Cliff Burnett (*Evener*)
Cliff trained at Lancaster University and E15 Drama School. Cliff has also worked extensively as a Theatre Director, including four years as Associate Director of Dundee Rep and later, Artistic Director of Durham Theatre Company. In 1998, Cliff set up his own company Theatre Of The Miraculous with whom he continues to develop film and theatre based projects. For the Traverse: *Accounts* (Traverse Theatre/Riverside Studios). Other theatre includes: *Romeo and Juliet, The Cherry Orchard, Equus, Moby Dick Rehearsed, The Tempest, Hedda Gabbler* (Dundee Rep); *Peer Gynt* (Dundee Rep/National Theatre of Scotland); *Othello* (Byre Theatre); *Gaslight, Abigail's Party, Absurd Person Singular* (Theatre by the Lake, Keswick); *Hapgood, Pygmalion, Taking Steps, Picture of Dorian Gray* (Century Theatre); *Genius, Bring Me Sunshine, A View From The Bridge, Dracula, The Merchant of Venice, Cabaret* (Newcastle Playhouse); *Romeo and Juliet* (Royal Shakespeare Company); *The Guise* (Royal Court Theatre). Film and television credits include *A Prayer for the Dying* (MGM); *Travels in Written Britain, Emmerdale* (ITV); *Bergerac, Mortlock of Cambridge* (BBC); *Shine on Harvey Moon, Last Place on Earth* (Central TV). Radio credits include *Break My Bones; Listen to The Singing, Epsom Downs, Accounts* (BBC Radio); *The Machine Stops, Hassan* (Metro Radio).

Darrell D'Silva (Pierre)
Theatre credits include The Rose Tattoo, Royal Hunt of the Sun, Tales from Vienna Woods, Closer (Royal National Theatre); Hecuba, A Midsummer Night's Dream, A Month in the Country, Troilus and Cressida, Camino Reale, The Spanish Tragedy, Henry VIII, Dr Faustus (Royal Shakespeare Company); Paradise Lost (Northampton Theatre); Franco Zefferelli's Absolutely! (Perhaps) (Wyndhams Theatre); The Lying Kind (Royal Court Theatre); Romeo and Juliet, The Three Musketeers (The Crucible, Sheffield); Six Characters in Search of An Author (Young Vic); Further Than the Furthest Thing (Tron Theatre/ Royal National Theatre); Crossfire (Paines Plough); Tear from a Glass Eye (Gate Theatre); Antarctica (Savoy). Television credits include Trial and Retribution (LaPlante Productions); Bonekickers, Criminal Justice, Krakatoa, Messiah, Cambridge Spies, Spooks, Out of the Blue (BBC); Saddam's Tribe, Poppy Shakespeare, Titanic, A Very British Sex Scandal (Channel Four); In Defence (ITV); To Be First (Discovery/Channel Four); Lawless (Company Pictures); Dinotopia (Thistle); Table Twelve: After Hours (World Productions); Prime Suspect (Granada); Wokwenwell (LWT); Faith (Central Films); Queen of Swords (Canada). Film credits include Dirty Pretty Things (Miramax).

Brian Ferguson (Guard)
Brian trained at RSAMD. For the Traverse: Rupture (co-production with the National Theatre of Scotland Workshop). Other theatre credits include The Drawer Boy, Love Freaks (Tron Theatre); They Make These Noises, Spanglebaby (Arches Theatre Company); Snuff (Arches Theatre Company/National Theatre of Scotland); Black Watch (National Theatre of Scotland); Falling (Poorboy/National Theatre of Scotland); Particularly in the Heartland (The TEAM); Bridgebuilders (Poorboy); Decky Does A Bronco (Grid Iron); Observe the Sons of Ulster (Citizens Theatre); She Stoops to Conquer (Perth Theatre). Film & Television credits include Voices (Phase IV Productions); Taggart: Island (SMG); Black Watch, River City (BBC); Still Game (Comedy Unit/BBC); Overnite Express (Square GO Productions/BBC); Last Legs (Stella Maris Films/STV); Rockface (Union Pictures/BBC).

Meg Fraser (Kiki)
Meg trained at RSAMD and was an original member of Dundee Rep Ensemble Company for 3 years with shows including The Winter's Tale (tour to Iraq), The Seagull, Cabaret, Mince, Changing Kevin's Story, The Night Before Christmas, A Family Affair, A Midsummer Night's Dream, Puss in Boots, The Princess and the Goblin. She was awarded the 2007 TMA Best Supporting Actress Award for her performance in All My Sons (Royal Lyceum Theatre, Edinburgh) and the 2007 Critics' Award for Theatre in Scotland, Best Female Performance for her

performance in *Tom Fool* (Citizens Theatre). For the Traverse: *Nova Scotia*. Other theatre credits include *The Night Before Christmas* (Coventry Belgrade); *Being Norwegian* (Paines Plough/Oran Mor); *Game Theory* (Ek Productions); *What I Heard About Iraq* (James Seabright/Paul Lucas Productions); *Eric La Rue* (Royal Shakespeare Company/Soho Theatre); *Twelfth Night, As You Like It, Hamlet, Macbeth, Young People's Macbeth* (Royal Shakespeare Company); *Julius Caesar, The Taming of the Shrew, The Playboy of the Western World* (Royal Lyceum Theatre, Edinburgh). Radio credits include *An Expert in Murder, The Tenderness of Wolves, The Trick is to Keep Breathing, Hand in Glove* (BBC). Film and television includes *Young Adam* (Studio Canal); *Taggart – Atonement* and *The Island* (SMG).

Zinnie Harris (Playwright)
Zinnie Harris is a playwright and theatre director living in Edinburgh. She read Zoology at St. Anne's College, Oxford and then took an MA in Theatre Production (Directing) at Hull University. Theatre credits include *Further Than the Furthest Thing* (Tron Theatre/Royal National Theatre) winner of the Peggy Ramsay Foundation Award 1999, Fringe First 2000, John Whiting Award 2000; *Miss Julie* (adapted for the National Theatre of Scotland); *Solstice, Midwinter* (Royal Shakespeare Company); *Nightingale and Chase* (Royal Court Theatre); *By Many Wounds* (Hampstead Theatre). Television credits include: *Born with Two Mothers, Richard Is My Boyfriend* (Channel Four); *Spooks* (BBC). Directing credits include *Miss Julie* (National Theatre of Scotland); *Solstice, Midwinter* (Royal Shakespeare Company); *Gilt* (7:84); *Dealer's Choice* (Tron Theatre); *Master of the House* (BBC Radio 4). Zinnie is currently Scottish Arts Council Senior Playwriting Fellow at the Traverse Theatre.

Paul Hickey (Howard)
Theatre Credits include *Fewer Emergencies, Crazyblackmotherfuckingself* (Royal Court Theatre); *O Go My Man* (Royal Court Theatre/Out of Joint); *Peer Gynt, Romeo and Juliet, Playboy of the Western World* (Royal National Theatre); *Protestants* (Traverse/Soho Theatre); *Drink, Dance, Laugh, Lie* (Bush Theatre); *In A Little World of Our Own* (Donmar Warehouse) *Pentecost* (Donmar Warehouse/Rough Magic) ; *Dealer's Choice, My Night With Reg* (Birmingham Rep); *The Merchant of Venice* (Royal Shakespeare Company); *The Deep Blue Sea* (Royal Exchange); *Red Roses and Petrol, The Ash Fire* (Tricycle); *Lady Windermere's Fan* (Rough Magic/Tricycle); *The Plough and the Stars, Aristocrats, The Silver Tassie, Howling Moon Silent Sons* (Abbey Theatre). Television credits include *Sunshine, Whitechapel, Murder Squad, The Governor, The Inspector Lynley Mysteries (Series IV, V & VI), Nuremburg, Friends and*

Crocodiles, Rebel Heart, The American, Father Ted, The Informant.
Film credits include *The Matchmaker* (Working Title); *Though the Sky Falls* (Irish Screen); *On the Edge* (Universal); *Saving Private Ryan* (Dreamworks); *Moll Flanders* (MGM); *Nora* (Natural Nylon); *The General* (K.B.S); *Ordinary Decent Criminal* (Miramax).

Dominic Hill (Director)
Dominic became Artistic Director of the Traverse Theatre in January, 2008. Before joining the Traverse, Dominic was Joint Artistic Director of Dundee Rep Theatre from 2003 – 2007. Previously, he worked as a freelance director, Associate Director at The Orange Tree Theatre (Richmond), Assistant Director at the Royal Shakespeare Company and Assistant Director at Perth Theatre (1994 – 1996). *Fall* is Dominic's first production for the Traverse. Productions for Dundee Rep Theatre include *Peer Gynt* (co-produced with the National Theatre of Scotland and winner Best Director, Best Actor, Best Design and Best Production, Critics' Awards for Theatre in Scotland 2008), *Happy Days, Hansel and Gretel, A Midsummer Night's Dream, Monkey, The Talented Mr Ripley, Ubu the King, The Graduate, Macbeth, Scenes from an Execution* (winner of Best Director and Best Production, Critics' Awards for Theatre in Scotland, 2003), *Peter Pan, Twelfth Night, Dancing at Lughnasa, The Snow Queen, The Duchess of Malfi* and *The Winter's Tale* (nominated for Best Director, Barclays/TMA Awards). Other directing credits include *Falstaff* (Scottish Opera); *A Prayer for my Daughter* (Young Vic); *Just Between Ourselves, So Long Life* (Bath Theatre Royal/Tour); *Romeo and Juliet* (Open Air Theatre, Regent's Park); *Five Finger Exercise* (Salisbury Playhouse); *The Danny Crowe Show* (Bush Theatre); *Betrayal, The Rivals* (Northcott Theatre, Exeter); *Spike* (Nuffield Theatre, Southampton/Theatre of Comedy); *The Diary of a Madman* (Royal National Theatre/Tour); *Passing Places* (Greenwich Theatre/Derby Playhouse); *The Rise and Fall of Little Voice* (Salisbury Playhouse); *Blithe Spirit, A Streetcar Named Desire* (Mercury Theatre, Colchester).

Dan Jones (Sound Designer)
Dan Jones is a British composer and sound designer working in film and theatre. His film scores include *Shadow of the Vampire* (starring John Malkovich and Willem Dafoe) and Menno Meyes' *Max* (starring John Cusack), for which he received the Ivor Novello Award for Best Film Score, 2004. He has written for all the major British television broadcasters, his work for TV including Sir David Attenborough's *The Life of Mammals*, the BBC series *Strange*, Pawel Pawlikowski's drama *Twockers* and Francesca Jospeh's *Tomorrow La Scala*. He collaborated with Sebastiao Salgado, John Berger, and Paul Carlin on the BBC Arena special *The Spectre of Hope*. Dan has also created music and soundscapes for large scale public artworks. He is the co-creator of

Sky Orchestra where music is played from seven hot air balloons positioned over a city, making it one of the largest soundscapes in the world. His music has also been used by the Rambert Dance Company, The European Space Agency and was incorporated in Issac Julien's *Paradise Omeros* which is exhibited at Tate Modern, London. He is a founder member and co-artistic director of Sound and Fury Theatre Company whose productions pioneer the immersive use of experimental sound design.

Kevin McMonagle *(Liddel)*

Kevin trained with the late Hugo Gifford in Glasgow and at Drama Centre London. He has been involved in New Writing most of his career and premieres of new work include that of the writers Peter Arnott, Simon Bent, Torben Betts, Ranjit Bolt, John Byrne, Caryl Churchill, John Clifford, Lucinda Coxon , Keith Dewhurst, Lucy Gannon, Alasdair Gray, Ian Heggie, Jim Kelman, Tom Leonard, Liz Lochhead, John McGrath, Graham McLaren, Gregory Motton, Klaus Pohl, Jeremy Raison, Jeremy Seabrook, Vassily Sigarev and Stephen Wyatt. Most recently he appeared in *Russian National Mail* by Oleg Bogaev at Theatre Doc, Moscow and The Ekaterinburg Festival, western Siberia. His last work with Zinnie Harris was *Further than the Furthest Thing* a Tron Theatre/Royal National Theatre Production in 2000.

Tom Piper *(Designer)*

Tom is the Associate Designer of the Royal Shakespeare Company and has designed extensively for the company with shows including *The Broken Heart, Spring Awakening, A Patriot for Me, Much Ado About Nothing, The Spanish Tragedy, Bartholemew Fair, Measure for Measure, Troilus and Cressida, A Month in the Country, A Midsummer Night's Dream, Romeo and Juliet, The Tempest, King Lear, Macbeth, Hamlet, Twelfth Night.* Tom has also designed many new writing pieces for the company, including *Midwinter* and *Solstice*, written and directed by Zinnie Harris. His most recent work was the Histories Cycle, featured as part of the Complete Works season which was seen at the Courtyard Theatre and the Roundhouse and included *Henry VI Parts 1–3, Richard III, Richard II, Henry IV Parts 1 and 2* and *Henry V.* Other designs include *Zorro* (West End/National Tour); *Dealer's Choice* (Menier Chocolate Factory/West End); *Falstaff, Macbeth* (Scottish Opera); *The Birthday Party, Blinded by the Sun, Oh! What a Lovely War* (Royal National Theatre); *Miss Julie* (Haymarket Theatre); *Frame 312, A Lie of the Mind, Three Days of Rain, Helpless* (Donmar Warehouse); *Pants, Mince, The Duchess of Malfi, Twelfth Night, Happy Days* (Dundee Rep); *Denial, Les Liaisons Dangereuses, Ghosts* (Bristol Old Vic); *The Danny Crowe Show* (Bush Theatre); *The Frogs, The Cherry Orchard* (Nottingham Playhouse); *Stiff!, The Master*

Builder (Royal Lyceum Theatre, Edinburgh); *The Crucible, Six Characters in Search of An Author* (Abbey Theatre); *Backpay, Cockroach, Who?* (Royal Court Theatre); *Waking Tulipfutures, Ripped, My Goat, Rockstation* (Soho Theatre); *Endgame, Dumbstruck, Macbeth* (Tron Theatre); *Insignificance* (Sheffield Theatre); *Head/Case* (Belgrade Coventry); *Babette's Feast* (Royal Opera House).

Chahine Yavroyan (Lighting Designer)

For the Traverse: *Damascus, Strawberries in January, When the Bulbul Stopped Singing, Outlying Islands, 15 Seconds, Iron, Green Field, Gagarin Way, Wiping My Mother's Arse, King Of The Fields, The Speculator, Danny 306+Me (4 Ever), Perfect Days, Kill The Old Torture Their Young, Anna Weiss, Knives In Hens, The Architect, Shining Souls.* Other theatre includes: *Relocated* (Royal Court Theatre); *Elizabeth Gordon Quinn, The Wonderful World of Dissocia, Realism* (National Theatre of Scotland); *San Diego, The Cosmonaut's Last Message to the Woman He Once Loved in the Former Soviet Union* (Tron Theatre); *Dalston Songs* (ROH2); *Mahabharata* (Sadler's Wells); *The Death of Klinghoffer* (Edinburgh International Festival); *House Of Agnes, Long Time Dead, After The End* (Paines Plough); *How To Live* (Bobby Baker). He has worked extensively in theatre, with companies and artists including: The Crucible; Royal Exchange; Nottingham Playhouse; Leicester Haymarket; Institute of Contemporary Arts; English National Opera; Lindsay Kemp; Rose English; Pip Simmons. Dance work with: Frauke Requardt Dance Co; CanDoCo; Yolande Snaith Theatredance; Bock & Vincenzi; Jasmin Vardimon; Anatomy Performance Company; Naheed Saddiqui, X Factor. Site Specific work includes *Ghost Sonata* (Sefton Pk. Palmhouse); *Enchanted Parks* (Leazes Pk. and Saltwell Pk.); *Dreams of a Winter Night* (Belsay Hall); *Deep End* (Marshall St. Baths) *Spa* (Elizabeth Garrat Anderson Hospital); *Sleeping Beauty* (St. Pancras Chambers). Fashion work includes shows for Givenchy; Chalayan; Clemens-Riberio; Ghost. Chahine is a long standing People Show person.

Samantha Young (Justine)

Samantha trained at RSAMD. Theatre credits include *I'll be the Devil* (Royal Shakespeare Company); *Hamlet, Snow White* (Citizens Theatre); *Europe* (Dundee Rep/Barbican); *Gobbo, Miss Julie,* (National Theatre of Scotland); *The Crucible* (TAG Theatre/National Theatre of Scotland); *A Taste of Honey* (TAG Theatre); *The Graduate, The Visit, A Lie of The Mind, Macbeth* (Dundee Rep). Film and television credits include *Casualty* (BBC); *River City* (BBC Scotland); *Mono* (Digicult/G.M.A.C). Radio work includes *Look Back in Anger, Almost Blue* (BBC Radio 4).

ARE YOU DEVOTED?

**Our Devotees are: Joan Aitken, Stewart Binnie,
Katie Bradford, Adrienne Sinclair Chalmers,
Adam Fowler, Joscelyn Fox, Anne Gallacher,
Keith Guy, John Knight OBE, Iain Millar,
Gillian Moulton,Helen Pitkethly, Michael Ridings,
Bridget Stevens, Walton & Parkinson**

The Traverse could not function without the generous support
of our patrons. In March 2006 the Traverse Devotees
was launched to offer a whole host of exclusive benefits
to our loyal supporters.

Become a Traverse Devotee for
£29 per month or £350 per annum
and receive:

- A night at the theatre including six tickets, drinks and a backstage tour

- Your name inscribed on a brick in our wall

- Sponsorship of one of our brand new Traverse 2 seats

- Invitations to Devotees' events

- Your name featured on this page in Traverse Theatre Company scripts and a copy mailed to you

- Free hire of the Traverse Bar Café (subject to availability)

Bricks in our wall and seats in Traverse 2
are also available separately. Inscribed with a message
of your choice, these make ideal and unusual gifts.

To join the Devotees or to discuss giving us your support
in another way, please contact our Development Department
on 0131 228 3223 / development@traverse.co.uk

TRAVERSE THEATRE – THE COMPANY

Zinnie Harris
Fall

ff

faber and faber

First published in 2008
by Faber and Faber Limited
3 Queen Square, London WC1N 3AU

Typeset by Country Setting, Kingsdown, Kent CT14 8ES
Printed in England by CPI Bookmarque, Croydon, Surrey

A CIP record for this book
is available from the British Library

ISBN 978-0-571-24514-7

2 4 6 8 10 9 7 5 3 1

For Malachy and Jasper, with hope

Fall is the last play in a trilogy of plays,
Solstice, *Midwinter* and *Fall*, and it can be seen
either alone or as part of the whole.

They all have a people, and all have a river.
Other than that, the setting may or may not
be the same.

Characters

Kate
a woman in her fifties, from the mountains

Evener
a war criminal

Liddel
a doctor, a friend of Kate's

Guard
a prison guard

Pierre
the Prime Minister

Kiki
his wife

Howard
his deputy

Justine
an activist from London

Act One

SCENE ONE

A prison cell.
A very old man and a woman in her fifties.
The old man, Evener, sits on a hard-backed chair.
The woman, Kate, on the floor.
Silence.
Then the woman begins to speak. Slowly at first.

Kate
I was listening to a record.
    Was interrupted by his footsteps. I had been waiting for him. Waiting for him and not waiting.
    Alone.
    You know what alone is.
    Only me and the fields.
    A magpie swooping over the house.
    A stray cat that came looking for milk.
    I was cooking beans.
    Or I should have been – I had cut the halves up and I remember because I had cut my thumb. I had to go looking for a plaster.
    He doesn't really like beans, but he tolerates it.
    He thinks we eat too many beans.
    I tried to tease him about it, but he never laughs.
    Work is a hard place.
    They put pressure on him. It's a horrible environment.
    I understand that.
    Everyone told me I had made a good match when I married him.
    It's funny because the first half of the evening is so clear and yet, later, I can't remember clearing away the

meal. Did we eat the beans in the end? We certainly hadn't eaten anything before the doorbell rang.

The beans were boiling. I remember that because I had to turn them off. A minute later, in the panic, I turned them off. They will boil over, I thought, strange how one has some presence of mind whatever the circumstance. There will be water all over the floor.

He answered the door.

It was Liddel. Our good friend. A doctor.

And we said come in, and he said he couldn't.

And Hal says, why man, don't be absurd, don't just stand there in the cold. Come in and put the door shut behind you.

I have blood on my shoes, says Liddel.

And I looked and sure enough there was blood on his shoes.

I've hit something, he says.

And Hal hasn't heard properly because he is still trying to get him through the door.

He has hit something, Hal, I say. In the car.

Liddel's voice is shaking.

I thought it was just a badger, but it's not.

Oh my God, that was me, but in my head. The inner voice in my skull, breathing. Oh my God, we are here already.

And I realise that is what I have been waiting for, all these months I have been waiting, and not knowing why I can't move from my chair hardly, just about make it to the end of the lane, but further? No. I have to be home because of the man Liddel will hit on our track.

I am kind of momentarily paralysed, but Hal and Liddel, they rush around. They take a torch and go out immediately. It's dark already.

I turn off the beans.

They are already boiling.

I look out of the window.

I can see the torch, the two men. They are standing over something, looking.

When Liddel comes back in, he is shaking. I pour him a brandy.

It is too late, he says.

Who was he? I ask.

No one, he says. No one we recognise.

Hal comes back in.

I need a sheet, he says.

An old one.

What are you going to do with it? Him?

I am sorry to describe it this way, but that is how it was.

I am going to wrap him in a sheet and throw him in the river.

Liddel is a good man, that is the basis we were working from. A good man, but not a good driver. He has caused an accident before and lost his licence. He shouldn't have been driving, we both had told him that many times, but he had to go to and from his mother's door, and out to the surgery three times a week. He had to drive.

The blood, where did the blood come from? I asked.

What blood?

The blood on your shoes. You are covered in blood, and yet even from the window I could see there was none on the man.

He had a dog. Liddel said.

The dog is still on the road.

I go to the cupboard to give Hal a sheet. I am not happy about it, I mean not the sheet. I would have given our best sheets, but I am not happy about Hal's plan. I ask him about it.

By the morning he will be out to sea, he says.

He is some mother's son, I say.

I can see that cloud over his face again, he doesn't want an argument.

People do worse, he says.

We are trying to be civilised now though, aren't we? I answer back. I know it sounds silly that I said that, but back then that was how we were thinking. I was thinking. I was conscious in everything we did, we had to try to break a mould. Think differently, approach things with a new gaze.

We will pick some flowers, Hal said.

Throw them in the river after him.

It is autumn, the flowers are dead, I said.

So is he. So is he, Kate.

He is completely DEAD.

Beat.

Liddel watching all the time.

He had seen me and Hal lots over the years, knew what we were like.

We disagree, it doesn't matter.

Hal goes on.

Know what we could do?

What most of the country would do?

Don't, I say.

Why not? Others would. All we'd have to do is strip him and shave him, and say we found him somewhere. OK, we might have to put a match up to his face, burn the skin a little, break a few bones, take away any distinguishing marks. Then we take him to the nearest grieving widow and we knock on her door.

There are so many desperate women out there, Kate, we won't have to look hard. And when she answers the door, she will look us in the face, and we will say, good news. Good news. We have found your old Tom Hindler or Sam Oldbody or whoever. We found him lying in a field or thrown from a prison or lynched from a tree. Look, here he is.

And the old dear is so split in two by the moment that her face almost goes as grey as the corpse itself. Don't look at me like that, Kate, I see this every day of the week. You wonder why I need a drink when I come in, I see this every day. And yet somehow, because they are amazing, these old women, most of them not even that old, somehow she has enough dignity instilled in her, from watching her mother and grandmother, that she knows she must have the presence of mind to feel into her pocket and pull out a few coins. A pound or two. A dollar. All she can afford.

And she'll press it into our hands and she will even thank us.

You might not like it. But read the papers. It happens every day. If you ever stepped out the door –

I know what goes on, I say.

Then don't talk about being civilised. Hal again. Don't think that all this talk of a new government means we are civilised.

And it is true if we were like our neighbours, a dead old man, newly mutilated, battered and shorn, would soon be lying in a grave belonging to a man he never heard of, and being visited every day by a woman he never met.

But we aren't like our neighbours, I say.

Exactly, says Hal, let's take him down to the river and send him out to sea.

Beat.

Maybe we ate the beans while we decided.

We got some brandy out, I know that. Liddel's hands still shaking.

Hal's face clouding over.

It's the curious thing about him, and I told him so. It's the thing I always forget and yet at the beginning I most loved.

He never asks for help.

He works for this new government, did. He was one of the people that hands out the new helpline numbers, the new initiatives they come from him. Or the department he worked in anyway. And yet when it comes to it – he won't call.

Liddel, he says, I told you. He will go to prison.

He doesn't even like Liddel. I should have realised then. Liddel if anything is my friend. I like having him around, just as a third person. Another person sitting in another chair. Stopping us being two.

If Hal had had his way, Liddel would have stopped calling years ago.

You make up another explanation of why we have a dead man on our drive and I will call. Hal again.

Liddel drinks his brandy.

I'll bury the dog, I say.

I pick up the shovel.

He doesn't try to stop me. Doesn't say, don't go out, stay in where it is warm.

He lets me go.

He must have been sure you were dead.

It's not all that cold. I'm sure you were freezing, but it was still a mild night. The week before we had had frost and so all the trees were losing their leaves, and I had said that to Liddel, while we were in the kitchen, there were leaves all over the roads, no wonder it was skiddy.

He didn't really answer.

He still hadn't taken off his shoes.

I followed his footprints back to the car.

I could see that he had walked round twice. It looked like he had got out once and got back into the car. Had maybe sat there thinking, what do I do next, or perhaps just sat there thinking nothing at all, like I do.

Hal and Liddel must have moved you, that was my first
thought. They must have moved you clear of the road,
because where you were and where the car was, they
didn't add up. You couldn't have been thrown that
wide.

They must have carried you carefully and laid you
down.

Like a little child. Asleep.

Only not, of course.

I had only seen one dead body before, and don't say
how did I manage that. I know I was lucky, in some
ways. Or lucky not to have seen. The people I lost were
taken away and shot and never returned, so one didn't
have to see them dead, didn't have to go to funerals
with open-topped coffins and stare at any dead faces.

The person I had seen was a dead child.

Died of a fever. Not the only child in the village to
get it, but the only to die. After all we have been
through, this, the mothers agreed.

I never touched her.

I went to the funeral and held her mother's hand but
never touched her.

I had wanted to.

Like I had wanted to touch my own.

So, you, you were intriguing.

Only you weren't dead.

I was reaching out to straighten up your shirt,
which had somehow got caught under you as they had
moved you, I suppose, and once I had done that, I was
intrigued, as I said, intrigued by how your skin would
feel, whether it would be clammy or still warm or just
cold. My hands are always freezing, but would they be
colder than yours?

I put my hand around your neck, and then further
down to your chest.

You were cold. Cold as the day.

On that score you felt as dead as you could be.

But somewhere under that ripped shirt and cold skin a frail heart was still beating.

I ran back to the kitchen, I was calling them from the path. Hal, Liddel, help help, he isn't dead. He is still breathing, his heart. Help we need help, we must call help.

Of course, that's it: that is when they were eating the beans. They had sat down and started eating the beans while I had gone to bury the dead dog.

They both came.

An alive man in your garden is a different kind of problem.

Yes, your heart was beating, but only vaguely. A beat every so often – I wouldn't call it strong. And God knows what other injuries you had.

Hal ran back to the phone. The helpline number. I don't know if he needed to look it up or if it just came into his head naturally.

It isn't working, he said.

Ironic really, on the day we needed it. We just got put in a queue and seemed to stay there. There is something wrong, Hal said. We shouldn't go through to this tune. This is the tune we have when you have reached the end of the line. You could be listening to that tune all night. The man needs help, I was saying, and quick.

I'll take him, says Liddel. I can put him in the back of the car, and drive him to the town.

Don't be ridiculous, I told him. Apart from the fact that he was still shaking, shouldn't be driving in the first place, Liddel had had most of the bottle of brandy since he had been in my kitchen. He couldn't go.

So I'll take him, said Hal.

And nobody disagreed.

It has crossed my mind, many times if you must know, that he didn't recognise you at all. Or at least not by that point. That he really was offering help. Intending to do just as he said.

But I don't think that was really how it was.

It would be nice to think that for a second, comforting, but I am trying to think differently now. About him anyway.

He must have recognised you the first moment he saw you. Musn't he?

And must have known what he had to do.

You would have recognised him, wouldn't you? If you had had your eyes open?

The old man makes no answer, although she seems to be requiring him to speak.

Would you have recognised him?

Evener
Are you talking to me?

Kate
Yes.

It looks as if that is all Kate is going to get out of him. Then:

Evener
It would depend how hard the car had hit him.

Kate
He has grown a beard.

Evener
It might have thrown me.

Kate
He is still as ugly as sin.

When he used to lie on top of me I would almost be retching.

Evener

Is that true?

Kate

I don't know, how the fuck should I know. I can't remember. Probably not.

What is truth now really, anyway? You want to tell me that?

I think about him lying on top of me and I want to retch.

Evener

Ah.

Kate

It comes to the same thing.

Evener

But at the time . . .?

Kate

He was a good fuck.
What can I say?

Beat.

Do you want me to stop, should I go?

Evener

If I say stay, you will go, and if I say go, you will stay, is that it?

Kate

Do you want me to stay?

Evener

No, I want you to go.

Kate

Then I will stay.

What do you think his plan would have been? You know him better than me. Drive you half a mile up the

road, slit your throat, then dump you in the river, as he
suggested before?

Evener shrugs.

Anyway, a second car came down the drive and that
changed all his plans.

Moussa and her husband.

They live next door, only next door up where we
are is about a mile away, so they always use their car
even though they could walk. They are too fat, the
pair of them, and walking would do them good, but
there we go.

Sometimes I wish I could go back to that moment,
just to see is there a trace, just a little whiff, or a look,
is there anything that comes over him? All this,
everything that we had, must have looked shaky to
him then. Surely? Not that we had much really, but . . .

In the end, Moussa's husband – can never remember
his name although I know him perfectly well – and
Hal drove you into town. Together. Hal could hardly
say no, could he? It was the only thing to do.

I buried the dog.

Your dog.

You don't need to thank me by the way for that.

I did it for the dog.

Evener
Merci.

Kate
And we went to bed, later I mean. When he had got
back from the town.

When Liddel had gone home.

He was completely normal.

He took off his shoes like he always did,
unbuttoned his shirt.

Got into bed.

Beat.

Does the window open in here? Don't you need air?

Beat.

Later that night the officials came back.

We were asleep.

The third car on our drive, we don't normally have cars on our drive, by the way. We hardly ever see anyone except Liddel.

The light from the headlamps came right across the room.

We went downstairs. He led the way. We opened the door.

It was an official, two of them, the second one was still getting out of the car. They sat down at our kitchen table, we turned a side light on, the main light was too bright for our sleepy eyes. They wanted to go over what had happened. Where exactly the man had been. We had expected this in a way, poor Liddel had expected it.

But the questions were going a different way.

They wanted to know what we had both been doing that day, all day.

They wanted to search the house.

The barn, the field.

They had brought a warrant.

Why, we asked.

Presumably he knew by now.

The man we found was wanted, they said. Wanted in connection with the war.

I felt a bit sick at that point. I remembered your fluttering heart.

They thought we might have been harbouring you, giving you house room. But of course they found nothing, no evidence of that.

By the time they left, it was almost dawn, I turned

20

the side light off. Neither of us were going to sleep again that night.

We went upstairs and made love.

We lay in each others arms, and talked about who you might be.

I thought they had found all they had wanted to find, I said to him. No, he said, there are still a few men on the loose, old generals high up in the army who when it was all over went into hiding. Evil, he said. I remember the word exactly.

What was he doing on our path?

Running, Hal said. What else was he doing?

You don't need to answer that now.

But I thought about it for the rest of the day, the week, the year. What were you doing on our path?

It's a good place to hide, that is what Hal said, up there, where it gets dark early. Plenty of old barns around.

Or was it Hal that you came for?

Beat.

Evener
Why are you here?
Did Silbermann send you, to torment me?
To find a way to get under my skin.

Kate
I call him Hal.
Please don't use that name.

Evener
Tell Silbermann to fuck off.

Kate
He is dead.

Beat.

Since you asked.

Just last week.
I don't know why he died, I don't know how.

Evener
He tied his shoelaces together.

Kate
Probably.

Evener
Or a guard, used his boot too forcefully?

Kate
I don't know.

Evener
Lucky bastard.

Beat.

Kate
Anyway, it is over for him.

Evener
So why the fuck are you coming to see me?

Kate
I . . .

Beat.

I need to know a few things.

Evener
I didn't know him.

Kate
You knew him better than I did.
I had been married to him for years and years, but you knew him better. As it turns out.

SCENE TWO

Outside in the square. Kate and another man, Liddel, sit on a bench.
Kate lights a cigarette.

Kate
God, I wish I could wash my hair and get the smell of that place off me.

Liddel
Nothing changes at home.

Kate
Oh.

Liddel
Since you ask.

Kate
I am sorry. Your mother?

Liddel
Still lives.
Unlike the cow.
You know the cow died?

Kate
I forgot.

Liddel
The stray cat has had kittens.

Kate
I thought it was a he . . .

Liddel
Seems not.

Kate laughs.

Kate

Moussa?

Liddel

Ah, there is a tale, she and her husband, they had a
fight.

Kate

She moved out?

Liddel

He moved out
At the weekend.

Kate

It won't last.

Liddel

Probably not.

Beat.

Come home.

Beat.

If not to the house, then come and live with me?

Kate

Not yet.

Liddel

Then when?

Kate

I don't know.

Liddel

It isn't healthy, being here, staying here.
And the city isn't safe, last night there were fires.

Kate

It seems it might be quick now.

Liddel

What do you mean?

Kate

They are clearing a space in the square.

Liddel

You are putting yourself through things.

Kate

I want you to get some things for me, if I make a list, there are some things in the house.

Liddel

It's boarded up.
    You asked me to board it up.

Kate

Take one of the boards down.
    Break in.

Liddel

I wish you would come home.

Kate

Have you got a piece of paper? I'll make a list.

Liddel

Kate?

Kate

I am listening, I hear you.
    Honestly, Liddel, I have heard you.
    And when I am ready, I will come.

Liddel

There is all this talk of trouble.
    Those fires last night were out of control.

Kate

I saw them.

Liddel

The city will be ablaze soon.

Kate

It's a few people letting off steam.

Liddel

You are safer in the country.

Kate

A piece of paper.

Liddel

Promise me you'll come home in the end.

Kate

I can't make any promises about anything.

Liddel

I'll marry you.

Kate

Don't be ridiculous.

Liddel

You know if you wanted, I would like a shot.

She looks at him.

Have I made a fool of myself?

Kate

Of course not.

Liddel

I am not talking about love.

Kate

What a pity, I thought you were.

Beat.

Liddel

I want you to be happy. I want you to start again, if
not with me then someone else.

Kate

I can't just forget him, I might like to, but I can't just –

Liddel

I am not saying you should.

Kate

There are some books upstairs.

In a box.

You might have to rummage around, look behind things, move whatever you have to. Listen I haven't got a pen, have you got one?

Liddel

Yes.

Kate

Then I will write them down.

There is a sketch pad somewhere.

It should be in the same box. And if you look in the drawer downstairs – don't look at me like that, I want you to listen to his. Downstairs in the second draw under the stairs, are some paints.

I also need some more clothes. I don't care what, go into my cupboard, take what you fancy.

Liddel

I'll buy you some new.

Kate

The old clothes are fine

I have an old green dress, I wore it before I was married. I would like that.

Liddel

OK.

Kate

I can't think of anything else.

A whole house, and nothing else I want.

If you can catch that stray cat I would love to see
him again.

Liddel
Her.

Kate
Her.

Liddel
Do you need any money?

Kate
No.

Liddel
Where are you staying?

Kate
In a hotel.

Liddel
And paying with what?

Kate
I haven't paid yet.

Liddel
Kate, you have to be sensible about this.

Kate
OK, I need some money.

Liddel
How much?

Kate
If I got his pension I would be fine, irony is.

Liddel
How much money?

Kate
I am not good with money.

Liddel
Then get good. I'll write you a cheque.
Either come home or grow up, Kate.

Beat.

Sorry, that was too harsh.

Kate
You were right though.

Liddel
I will give you a hundred.
When I see you next week you can have more.

Kate
Thank you.
I'll pay you back.

Liddel
I don't need you to.
If I had talked of love would it have made a difference?

Kate
You didn't.

Liddel
No, I didn't.

Kate
I should go.

Liddel
Not yet.
There were some things in the post that you need to deal with.

Kate
Oh.

Liddel gets a parcel out.
He puts it on the table.

Liddel

I didn't know whether to bring it.

She looks at it.

I'll put it away, I just wanted you to know I have it. It is there.

It's in my bag, I will keep it for you until you want it.

He doesn't take it.
She looks at him.
She opens the parcel.
In it is a shirt and a watch.
She takes them out.
She smells the shirt.
She puts them back in the parcel.

Kate

You have them.

Do what you want with them.

Beat.

People recognise me in the street now, you know, they either smile pityingly or they cross the road to the other side. You know that? Sometimes they speak to me, sometimes they spit.

She laughs, not that it is funny.

Fame. Of sorts.

Liddel

I saw him.

Kate

When?

Liddel

Last week. The night before.

We didn't talk.

Kate
Why are you telling me this?

Liddel shrugs.

Liddel
You aren't the only person he duped.

Beat.

Kate
Take the fucking parcel, you deal with this your way.
I'll deal with it mine.

Liddel
Take care of yourself then.

Kate
You swine.

She picks up her stuff and walks off.

Liddel
Kate?

Kate
I mean it, Liddel, don't try and tell me how to do it.
Don't try and get inside my head.

Liddel
I'll see you next week. I'll bring your green dress.

SCENE THREE

The prison cell.
A Prison Guard is clearing some things.
Kate comes in the door.

Kate
Oh.

Guard

He won't be long.
  Downstairs, they are just doing some checks.
  Come in if you want.

Kate

What sort of checks?

Guard

Search me.
  Can't see what difference it makes if he is well or
not, but there you go. He probably has raised blood
pressure, and so that means the doctor has to be
called, something like that. This place is different these
days, used not to be like this. Can't remember a doctor
ever being called before.
  Come in. I won't bite. By the way, this is just a job.
I'm quite nice really.

She comes in.

Take a seat. Make yourself at home.

She sits down, gingerly.

I could get you some tea, only I have to clear up in
here. The old man shat himself this morning.

Kate

Oh.

Guard

Think he did it on purpose, think he did it just to wind
me up.
  Do you think that?

Kate

I don't know.

Guard

I don't get wound up easy anyway, so that is something.

You have got to have a strong nerve to work here,
strong nerves and a steady hand.

Bloody hell, this stinks.

You sure you want to visit him today?

Kate

How is he?

Guard

Fucked if I know.

The old man, Evener, comes back in.

You little shit.

What you go and done all this for?

*The Guard holds the soiled sheet up in his face. Rubs it
in.*

What the fuck is this about?

He gets him to the floor.
Stamps on him with his big boots.
Once, twice.
*Then a third time that sounds like it will have broken
something.*
Speaks to Kate.

Stop him from doing it again, anyway.

Nice to chat to you.

Give us a knock if you want that tea.

The Guard leaves.
The old man is on the floor.
Pause.
Kate gets off the chair. She puts a hand out to him.

Evener

You shouldn't be here.

Kate

Take my hand.

Evener

I would rather you fucked off.

Kate

He must have broken your shoulder.

Evener

Does it matter?

He gets up of his own accord.
He sits on the bed.

I am a sociopath. And I have a broken shoulder.

Kate

I should report him.

Evener

Don't make me laugh. You see the space outside the window now. They have started putting posts into the ground. That is progress, isn't it? We are getting somewhere at last.

Beat.

Kate

I have brought a book.
I want you to read it.

Evener

Please.
I'll say what you want me to say about Silbermann, I'll describe him however you want, that he was misguided, that he was evil even, that he was innocent, but please leave me alone.

She gets the book out of her bag.

I don't know what you are trying to do, but it is folly. That is a very good word for it. What? Do you think you can save me? Read me your books and turn me back into a whole human being? I am not your husband, I hardly knew him.

Kate

That's not true.

Evener

I don't have the answers.

Yes, yes is the answer. You are foolish.

Beat.

And on top of foolish. Lost.

You remind me of my daughter if you must know.
She was another fuck-wit.

Not that she is here, interestingly.

Listen, if you want to bring me something, bring me
cigarettes. And you could open your legs if you want
to please me.

Lie on the bed, let me fuck you.

See, I am horrible, that is what you came to discover,
isn't it?

Kate

I don't believe you are.

Evener

Then you are even more stupid than you are ugly.

And you are ugly, believe me. I would only be
fucking you to do you a favour. You said you had
children – what, did you have to pay someone to screw
you? And what are the kids like, mini-midgets,
bearded dwarfs with disfigured faces, humpbacked
with faeces for brains?

Kate

Shut up.

Evener

Hit me.

Kate

No.

Evener
Then I won't stop.
I'll tell you about the time Silbermann flayed a whole family.
Just for the hell of it, just to see the parents scream as the kids were skinned in front of them.

She hits him.

That is better.
Everyone that comes into the room hits me.
Normally harder.

Beat.

I'm sorry, lady, I can't help you.

Beat.

Kate
I don't have children.
We, Hal and I . . .

Evener
He always had a small dick.
You want a child, you come to me.
Anyway, I would be thanking my lucky stars if I were you.

Kate
I have got some questions.

Evener
Will you suck me off if I answer them?

Kate
Stop this.
Please.

Beat.

I will leave if you answer them. I won't come back.

Evener

If I thought that was the case I might consider it. If I thought that it was possible to give you what you want, but I know women like you, you get this notion into your head. You think you know what being a person is. And you will need to go on and on until you can square it. It is like a puzzle, it will drive you insane. And an insane person doesn't keep their promises.

I don't have the key. He was one thing to you, he was another to me.

Kate

Eight questions. I have written them down.

Evener

You are intolerable, you know that, you are worse than the life sentence, if I had any strength I would break your neck.

Kate

Where did you meet?

Evener

Do you promise you will disappear?

Beat.

See, you can't even do that.

Kate

I promise.

Evener

We met in a training camp. Next.

Kate

How old were you?

Evener

I was forty-five. Silbermann –

Kate

Could you call him Hal?

Evener

Nope.

Not part of the bargain.

Kate

OK, Silbermann.

Evener

Was I don't know young, seventeen, eighteen.

I was running the camp.

He didn't have a beard in those days. I can't really remember, it was a while ago.

Kate

What was he like?

Evener

Um . . .

He was young, I guess. He was in the army, just joined. A good new recruit was always something one had one's eye kept out for, someone you could promote.

Kate

To do terrible things.

Evener

No, we weren't thinking like that.

We were thinking about the war.

Kate

He told me he was an apprentice at seventeen. To a tailor. He told me he spent most of the war making suits, uniforms.

Evener

He tells a good story, what can I say.

He was good with a gun, you could see that even on the first day. We took them out to an old disused site, gave them some target practice. Silbermann got it every time.

Kate

What was he like?

Evener

I told you.

Kate

No – to sit with, to share a meal with?

Evener

He was one of many. I didn't really know him well
until later.

Kate

When later?

Evener

When we were both based in the mountains.

He screwed a lot of the locals, is that what you
want to hear?

Kate

All young men do.

Evener

True.

But he was a ladies' man, small dick and all.

Kate

OK.

Evener

He was ambitious. If you want to know what it was,
where it started, it could have been that.

You gave him a job, he did it.

Dependable.

Kate

I agree.

You could rely on him.

Evener

Always.

Kate

When did you move to the mountains?

Evener

Er, I don't know, I was in my fifties.

Kate

And he was thirty.

Evener

Something like that.

Kate

He got promoted.

Evener

He had a good year.

He was good in charge of the men. We all had known that he would be.

He was good with people.

Strangely.

His people loved him.

You probably can relate to that.

Kate says nothing.

We needed someone ruthless. Someone who would go just that little bit further. We could see that there were going to be tough calls ahead. It looked like the insurgency was getting out of hand, there was talk of out-and-out war. Plus the internationals were starting to swoop around, we needed someone that could make a decision and see it through.

So we set him a test.

He had a good friend, Lulah they called him, I can't remember now what the hell his real name was. I'll think of it in the middle of the night probably. Anyway, this guy and Silbermann, they were young, they had a good time.

We decided to set Lulah up.

There was some rules in the camp, rules you didn't break. Stealing from each other was one of them. You have to understand that, out there, you have nothing but each other. So it is important that the guys trust each other.

We have to build up trust above everything else. And Silbermann was an officer by then, he had to enforce it.

We made it look like Lulah had been stealing supplies.

More than just supplies. Precious things from the other men.

We made it look like he was trading.

Trading stolen things.

We put Silbermann on to it. Lulah is a weasel, we said. His best friend, the intensity between them, it was almost like a love affair.

Silbermann had to deal with it. The evidence was overwhelming.

We had done our jobs.

He did his.

Kate
What does that mean?

Evener
What do you think?
Don't look like that, you can't pretend to look surprised that we were bastards.

Kate
Did Hal ever find out?

Evener
Find out what?

Kate
That you set him up.

41

Evener

Oh, wait a minute.

No, hang on.

He did find out, the guy I am thinking about did find out. Shit, sorry. I am thinking of another man. Not Silbermann. I always did used to get them mixed up. Sulleyman. We did all that to another guy, but Silbermann, no, I remember him now. He didn't need that kind of training, he was always a monster.

Kate

You cunt.

Evener

I told you, you wouldn't get answers from me.

Kate feels foolish. She picks up her book.

Go and live the rest of your life.

Don't try to find the place that we all lived in.

I can see you are a good woman, I didn't mean all that about being ugly.

Just leave this.

Kate

I can't.

Evener

Then no one can help you.

SCENE FOUR

A small ante-room.
Kiki and Pierre are getting ready to go out.
Kiki is putting on her accessories and looking at herself in the mirror.

Pierre

You look fabulous.

Kiki

You didn't even look.

Pierre

I don't need to, you always look fabulous.

Kiki

But in particular?

Pierre

In particular, delicious.
Edible.
Like a fruit tart.

Kiki

Too much then.

Pierre

No, not at all.

Kiki

I want to look serious.

Pierre

You look serious.

Kiki

I want to look sober, and intellectual and like I am
a woman of weight.
I should change my shoes, right?

Pierre

I wish you were just happy as you are.

Kiki

The fluffy, edible Kiki.

Pierre

No, the serious, sombre, intellectual Kiki that is
so confident about who she is that she doesn't need to
worry about what people think of her.

Kiki

I wish we didn't have to change in here. I wish we had had time to get home and change.

I feel like we live out of a suitcase.

Pierre

It would take too long.

Kiki

They could have sent a car.

Pierre

There is trouble in the city.

Kiki

What sort of trouble?

Pierre

I am not sure. Another fire.

No doubt I will hear tomorrow, there will be a report on my desk.

Kiki

We might as well be travelling salespeople living out of a suitcase.

Pierre

I quite like it.

Kiki

Do you?

Pierre

Yeah, it feels like the old days.

Kiki snorts.

Kiki

This might have been what you were doing in the old days, I sure wasn't.

Beat.

Who is going to be there?

Pierre

Boring people.

Kiki

Intellectual sombre boring people?

Pierre

Yes.

Kiki

I'll change my shoes.

Beat.

Pierre

Actually I don't know who will be there. In the particular. I know it is lots of people we should be nice to. Or I should say that will be nice to us. They probably despise us, me, behind our backs.

It's me who should be worried about what people think.

Kiki

Everybody loves you.

Pierre

At the moment, maybe.

Kiki

Of course they do.

Pierre

Fragile is the line between love and hate.

Kiki

You are their top man.

Pierre

Their deliverer.

Kiki

Yes.

Pierre

They think I can produce miracles. They think I am capable of getting this sodden country out of its hole.

Kiki

You are.

Pierre

Don't be ridiculous.

This country is fucked.

I am just stupid enough to give it my best shot.

Kiki

You always knew it was going to be like this.

Pierre

They think I am a conjurer, they think I can do no wrong.

Kiki

You have been pretty good so far.

Pierre

I have been lucky.

Kiki

You give them what they want.

Pierre

I have a massive overspend.

Kiki

Do we have to talk about this now?

Pierre

That is what you always say. I have to comment on your necklace when you ask, but when I need to talk about the overspend –

Kiki

You have kept the peace.

Pierre

Just.

Kiki

It is all anybody cares about.
    Everything else is detail.

Pierre

It's the particular.

Kiki

OK, it's the particular.

Pierre

I have kept the peace by the massive overspend. That's
the particular. All the money has gone into initiatives.
That is all anyone is doing, keeping the peace.
    Meanwhile the infrastructure, the fabric of what
keeps this place together –

Kiki

Can't we talk about this later?

Beat.

Pierre

Sure.

Kiki

You'll manage it, you always do.

Pierre

Yep.

Someone knocks at the door: another politician, Howard.

Howard

Sorry to disturb you. Hi, Kiki.

Kiki

Hi.

Howard

Just thought I should run over what we need to discuss.

Pierre

I thought it was a social thing.

Howard

It is, but there is going to be some work stuff, obviously, that is why they have you here. Is she wearing that?

Pierre

I think so, yes.

Kiki

What's wrong with it?

Howard

Nothing, it just –

Kiki

Too much?

Pierre

It looks fine.

Howard

It is a work thing, I think we should be clear.

Pierre

A work thing with wives.

Howard

Men like Malacont, they like to bring their wives, sure, but that doesn't mean it isn't business. Yes, Kiki, those other ones.

Pierre

I have a bit of a headache.

Howard

I'll get some aspirin, but the main thing is just to try to field their questions.

Pierre

No, I mean it is really quite a bad headache.
I'm not sure if I can go through with tonight.

Howard

Good joke. Now this associate of Malacont's, we have
managed to get him to come here only because we said
we'd consider anything.

Pierre

What if I said that, though, one day? That I couldn't
go through with it, would the sky fall, I mean, what?

Howard

Is he OK?

Kiki

Seemed fine earlier.

Howard

Hasn't missed a meal?

Pierre

It is an interesting question, though, isn't it? How
much can everything depend on my being there? What
if I really did get struck down right now with a
migraine, flashing lights, nausea, the whole thing,
what would you do?

Howard

Is this a serious question?

Pierre

Yes.

Howard

I would take your head, dunk it in that toilet and tell
you not to be such a fuck-wit.

Pierre

Under what circumstance would I not have to go?

Howard

You put yourself up for this, you went into this job,
You knew what it would entail.

Now don't be such a bloody idiot, and do your tie
again because it isn't straight.

Beat.

Pierre

I am not up to it.

Howard

Don't be so fucking absurd.

Pierre

The job is too big.

Howard

You think I don't know that?

You think my job is any easier?

Pierre

You get to have a headache when you want to.

Howard

No I don't.

None of us do, if we are going to get this sodding
country back on the rails, then no headaches.

Pierre

We won't do it.

Howard

Maybe not.

Pierre

Everything it ever had has been stripped out of it, what
is left no one wants, and most of the workforce is dead
or maimed. Added to that, there is no aid coming in,
and someone has told the country that it is being run
by a magician.

Howard

Well, that wasn't me.

Pierre

I really do have a headache now.

Howard

And I really will dunk your head in the toilet.

Kiki

I'll get an aspirin.

Howard

And you and I will sit down and I'll tell you about these men.

Pierre

No.

Howard

This is unacceptable. Pierre, this absolutely cannot happen. Do you know how hard I had to work to get Malacont and his men to even come here tonight? Kiki can get the fucking aspirin.

Pierre

If I get the aspirin I can get some air.

If I can get some air, I can consider going through with tonight. If I go through with it, then I won't have to ring and tell them I have a headache.

Howard

This is eight billion dollars of investment we are talking about.

Pierre

So let's not disappoint them.

Beat.
Pierre goes.
Howard and Kiki left.

Howard

Take off those damn shoes please, Kiki.
And the skirt – for God's sake, you look like a tart.
What the fuck is going on with him?

Kiki starts to change.

Kiki

I don't know.

Howard

We have got to keep him together. That is our priority.
Work is stressful, so home must be calm. Yes?

Kiki

OK.

Howard

Sex if he wants it, if he doesn't too bad.
For you, I mean.
Don't exhaust him just for your own ends.

Kiki

Sure.

Howard

And report back to me. Every day if necessary.
I want a full résumé of his physical and emotional
condition – a shit if he done a shit, why he is
constipated if he hasn't.

Kiki

He'll be fine.

Howard

It scares the hell out of me.

Beat. Some solidarity between the two of them.
Pierre comes back in.
He indicates, 'OK, I am ready.'
*Howard picks up his papers. Nothing is said about what
has gone on before.*

The last time Malacont was in the country, he was sounding optimistic. He had his reservations of course, mainly about internal security, but we have some statistics now, statistics that might reassure him. Kiki should try to chat to his wife as well.

Pierre
There was a woman downstairs.

Howard
And here – if you could just glance at these papers so the statistics trip off the tongue, particularly the crime reduction.

Pierre
There was a woman downstairs.

Howard
There are a whole load of women downstairs.

Pierre
She said she wanted to see me.

Howard
Who exactly are we talking about?

Pierre
I don't know.

Howard
We have an intruder, is that it?
Kiki, go and deal with it, would you?

Pierre
No.
Stay where you are, and why did you take off that skirt? I bloody loved it.

Howard
Listen, I really think you should eat something, I think this whole bloody attitude is probably because your

blood sugar is low or something, I'll get someone to make you a sandwich.

Pierre
I want you to let her talk to me.

Howard
Is she a journalist?

Pierre
I don't think so.

Howard
Has she got an agenda?

Pierre
I have no idea.

Howard
Have you learnt anything from your time in office?
Kiki, please put down that damn skirt and keep the old one on.

Pierre
Leave her alone, she is just being herself.

Howard
You are a politician, Pierre, she is your wife. Don't think this is about being yourself. Yourselves? Don't make me laugh. You are a construct, the pair of you. We invented you to get the votes. More important than the votes, to get the trust of the international community. You are so far from real people, I can't even describe to you –

Pierre
That is the problem, then.
And there is a real person downstairs, and I would like to meet her.

Beat.

Howard
Do you want me to resign? Is that what you are politely trying to say? You don't want my help any more?

Pierre
I am just talking about half an hour.
A slight change to the schedule.

Howard
She could have a bomb.

Pierre
So we can search her.
I have decided to meet her, Howard, with or without your blessing. You are my adviser, I have listened to your advice, but I have decided, this once, possibly on account of my headache or maybe on account of the fact that I haven't eaten much or just possibly because I am extremely tired, to bugger the schedule and see a woman who has no appointment, that will have no chance of ever getting an appointment because I am kept as far away from real people as possible.
Resign if you want to.

Howard
OK, I resign.

Pierre
Don't be so bloody stupid, I need you.
I'm only talking about half an hour.
Take Kiki, I'll be there.

Howard
I would do anything for you, you know that.

Pierre
I know that.

Howard
But you have to tell me what is going on.

Pierre

I am not up to the job, that is what is going on.

Howard

Don't be so stupid, if you can't do it, who the hell can?
Think about that. Come on, Keeks.

Pierre is left alone.
He looks into the mirror and straightens his tie.
He calls down on the phone.

Pierre

Send her up.

He tidies up the accessories that Kiki has left all over the place.
He sits down.
A knock at the door.
A young woman, Justine, enters, looking slightly apprehensive.
She has a shabby briefcase with her.

Justine

I am sorry, I am a bit under-dressed, I didn't really
think I would get this far, to be honest.

We work a rota system. Every day one of us tries to
get an appointment with you, we stand outside the
window with a placard, and today it was my turn.

No one has ever got anything like as close before.

Pierre

What can I say, you are lucky.

Do you want something to drink?

Justine

Are you having something?

Pierre

I don't drink. I am not supposed to drink.

I am going to have a fucking huge brandy.

Justine

OK.

I'll have one too.

I'm not even sure I have all the right papers.

It's a kind of exercise, publicity stunt, I didn't really think –

Pierre

Don't worry.

You don't have to talk.

If you want we can just have a drink.

Justine

Are you kidding?

This could make my career.

Pierre

If a career is what you want, fine.

He hands her the drink.

I don't even know which organisation you are from.

Justine

Sorry. I'm Justine, and I work for Prisoners Action.

Pierre

OK.

Justine

We are an international organisation, promoting justice particularly, but also –

Pierre

You don't think we should be executing our criminals.

Justine

In essence.

Here is a card.

Pierre

I recognise the logo.

Justine

We were there all the time, during the trials, we got a really good pitch outside the court.

Pierre

I am going to have another brandy, what about you?

Justine

I shouldn't.

Pierre

Why not?

Justine

OK, another one.

He pours the brandy.

Pierre

I was hoping you would be different, to be honest. You looked like such a real person, I was hoping that we could make a connection.

Justine

I don't really know how to take that.

Pierre

I don't want more people bringing business cards.

Justine

It's my job.
     Sorry.
     I get paid by the hour, to stand outside your railings.

Pierre

Maybe that is why you are different. You are naive. You think that you can get an appointment with me just by turning up.

Justine

I don't think that.
     It's a job.

Pierre
You are different, though.
    Different to the people in here. You look like
beneath your skin there is proper blood.

Justine
Are we having a meeting or not?

Pierre
OK, yes, let's have it.

Justine
I have a petition.

Pierre
Always a petition.

Justine
There is no doubt in anyone's minds that the people
that we are talking about need to be punished,
of course they do, and they represent the very worst of
humanity, but our organisation, and others, just wants
to pose the question, what do we do if we kill them?
Aren't we just repeating the same mistakes?
    There is a lot of clamouring for blood at the
moment, I understand that.

Pierre
Excuse me.

Justine
What?

Pierre
You have a . . .

Justine
What?

Pierre
You have a caterpillar crawling up your shirt.

Justine looks down.

Justine

Oh.

Thanks.

Pierre

It's OK.

Justine

This is serious. If you aren't in the mood I could come back another time?

Pierre

You won't get an appointment.

Justine

I thought you were the man to see. I thought you were the one that could help us if anyone could.

Pierre

Do you speak French?

Justine

What sort of question is that?

Pierre

Just interested.

Justine

Yes I do. As it happens.

Pierre

Good French?

Justine

Pretty good. You aren't going to help me at all, are you? You aren't even going to listen.

Pierre

I thought you were going to be somebody different.

I made a mistake.

Justine
Who was I going to be?

Beat.

I have followed you, your whole career. When you got
your first interview in the press I celebrated. I liked
what you said. What you thought. It made sense to me.
Getting an appointment with you was the worst
thing that could have happened to me.

Pierre
You are not from here, are you?

Justine
What sort of question is that?
My parents are.

Pierre
Where were you brought up?

Justine
Various places.
London.
I came back last year.

Pierre
You were going to be lovely.
You asked me who I thought you were going to be.
Someone lovely.
Warm.
Someone who would maybe hold my head.
Someone who would speak French perhaps. Quietly.
Someone I could just talk to person to person, two
people.
Like if we met at a bus stop.
In a park.
Like in the old days.

Justine

The old days, I don't know what the fuck you were doing in the old days. Most people I talk to were sitting in a sewer hoping to fuck they were going to be hit because then at least it would be over.

Pierre

At least it was real.

Justine

You need a psychiatrist.

Pierre

That is what my advisers think.

Justine

Take their advice.

She picks up the papers.

What about this?
    What should I tell my organisation?

Pierre

What is the biggest decision you have ever made?

Justine

Me?

Pierre

Yes.

Justine

I'm not sure.

Pierre

Are you married?

Justine

I have a boyfriend.

Pierre

Will you marry him?

Justine
I haven't decided yet.

Pierre
OK.

Justine
I have made decisions, of course I have.

Pierre
Like what?

Justine
What course to take at college.

Pierre
OK.

Justine
What to spend money on, where to live.

Pierre
Have you ever made a decision that involved another person?
Radically.
Think about it.

Justine
I chose a school for my sister.

Pierre
How was it?

Justine
It didn't work.

Pierre
How did it feel?

Justine
Terrible.

Pierre

We are getting somewhere.
Think again.

Pause.

Justine

I don't think I have. Sorry, not big ones.

Pierre

Lucky, lucky you.

That's why your head doesn't ache.

I would love, let me tell you something – what was your name, Justine – I would love to stand over there with a placard, getting paid by the hour, hoping to get an appointment with someone I could pass the buck to. I would love to go home at the end of that day, to the flat that I chose, and curl up and go to sleep. Do you think I could do that, Justine? Go and sleep in your flat?

Justine

I'm in a hotel.

Pierre

Hotel, then. Sorry, you don't need to look at me like that, I am not going completely off the deep end. I will look at your petition. Just leave it on the desk.

Justine

Will you?

Pierre

Of course I will.

She takes it out of her bag.

What would you do?

Justine

About what?

Pierre

About the old regime. The war criminals we have
sitting in our prisons.

Justine

I wouldn't kill them.

Pierre

You would tell that to the victims?

Justine

Yes, it isn't the right thing to do.

Pierre

Even the sisters, mothers, brothers, the people who
had been maimed? And everyone takes it, no riots in
the streets, no arson on government buildings? I am
part of a system, you know that, Justine. And this
system is trying to change very slowly. It's not
unreasonable that they feel this way, I am not going
to be the person that tells them that it is unreasonable.
To believe that is to have no imagination.

Justine

I have plenty of imagination.

Pierre

So you call it, then. You tell them how it is/going to be.
I will give you the mandate to cancel all the
executions. If you like.

Justine

How could I do that?

Pierre

Just by saying it.

Justine

Are you being serious?

Pierre

Are you ready for some responsibility? Some consequence? Some dirty fucking complex stuff with no right outcome? Maybe I am going mad here, but there are precedents for it, after all – didn't Pilate let someone from the crowd make a decision? Maybe he had a headache that day too. I am being serious now. It's your decision but to make it you must choose with full knowledge. In the particular. It is always in the particular that is tricky.

They were masters of cruelty, Justine, a cruelty that you cannot imagine. That is why you can't pass comment on this situation until you know what it is you are talking about.

Pause.

It was nice meeting you, there is the door.

Justine

What are you saying, you can't live through something and remain civilised?

Pierre

I am saying it is hard. It can't be imposed. An imposition is just another form of tyranny.

Justine

I realise that.

Pierre

Goodbye, Justine.

Justine

How long would it take?

Pierre

Would what take?

Justine

How long would it take for me to understand?

Pierre

It would depend on how much you could stomach at one time.

We have files. Tapes. Eye-witness reports. Correspondence from the condemned themselves. Bones, photos. It would take years. Sorry. The executions are on Thursday, forget it. It's impractical. I'm sorry, I have these ideas, I get carried away.

Beat.

Justine

You aren't being serious anyway, are you?

Pierre

I haven't thought this through, as you can imagine. I didn't expect you to stay.

I didn't expect any of this. God, I was only trying to get out of a drinks party.

Justine

I am not someone that shirks a challenge.

Pierre

I will know that about you for next time.

Pause.

Justine

Will you pour me another brandy?

Pierre

Of course.

He pours her another brandy.
She drinks it back in one go.
She comes over to him, puts her hands on either side of his ears.

What are you doing?

Justine

I'm holding your head.

SCENE FIVE

Kiki is sitting on a chair. Howard is fussing over her. Pierre has just walked into the room and got Howard's attention.

Howard

Brilliant, brilliant.

Pierre

Can't you tell a mistake when you see one?

Howard

How can you say that?

Can you just put these in your ears, Kiki, please?

Pierre

I was drunk when I sent you that memo.

Howard

It's the best piece of political thinking I have seen all year and you say it is a mistake? It's brilliant, Pierre, fucking brilliant. I want to rip your clothes off and bugger you senseless.

Pierre

Listen, please just imagine I never sent it, you were right, I was in a strange mood.

Howard

It's why you are running the country and I am running you, it's genius. (*To Kiki.*) Now would you be comfortable if you had to sit there for a couple of days?

Pierre

I didn't mean it.

Howard

It's too late.

Pierre
What do you mean?

Howard
I've just come from a press conference.
It's all arranged. There has been a temporary stay of execution, a postponement.

Pierre
No –

Howard
The press are all lined up to meet this woman.

Pierre
Oh God.

Howard
I have already sold her as the people's representative.
It's a kind of new democracy, born right here, and you invented it.

Pierre
She is just a girl.

Howard
Even better, she will strike the world as purer.
Kiki and I are just getting the practical details sorted, where she will sit and how she will listen. The tapes are arriving this morning.

Pierre
Have you gone mad?

Howard
I am thinking of having a glass box made so she can be in her own little world.

Pierre
Please stop this.

Howard

It was your idea.

Pierre

Tell me you are joking.

Howard

Why would I joke?

Pierre

You're pissed off about last night and this is some
elaborate payback.

Howard

No.

It's better than that. It's very simple.

No one would touch us, now they might.

Pierre

What are you talking about?

Howard

Our human rights record. Continental investment and
the OHF, they couldn't be seen to deal with us. But
now we get to say, look, it isn't us, the government's
name's on the death warrants, we the government are
changing, modernising, but the people, or this woman
as a representative of the people, have made their own
choice. And choice is the essence of democracy. We are
arguably more democratic than all of Europe. Think
of that.

Pierre

They will see through it.

Howard

Of course they will, but it doesn't matter. It's the
official line that counts. All they need is a way to get
us back around the table without risking their own
favour.

Pierre

They want us round the table?

Kiki

Can I go?

Howard

Not just yet, Keeks.

Pierre

This is all coming out of the blue for me.

Howard

Malacont has been our go-between, it's been
something of his idea.

We don't have anything we can sell, no minerals, no
resources, but we have space. And we have a blind eye.

Kiki

Only I have got stuff to do.

Howard

Before I go any further, just to say it isn't just
continental investment, it's everyone behind them,
right up to various European politicians.

Kiki

Please can I go?

Howard

Just another couple of minutes.

Pierre

What do they want?

Howard

A canal.

Pierre

A canal?

Howard

Alright, a canal and a factory.

Look, we don't ask.

A canal and a factory, for the investment that we need? For cheap fuel, for jobs and some sort of functioning economy?

We are talking about a thin strip of water, and a plot of land.

Pierre
Where is this canal?

Howard
Between the mountain and the border.

Pierre
You move the mountain?

Howard
I would call it a hill.

Pierre
You move a hill?

Howard
We cut through it, yes.

Pierre
What does the factory make?

Howard
That is where our valuable blind eye comes in.

Pierre
It's always ugly in the end.

Howard
It's eight billion dollars' worth of investment.

Pierre
But where does it end?
What else do we do because these investors want it?

Howard

We take our names off the death warrant and stick some woman's name there instead.

It makes everyone easier, that's all.

And the money easier.

It's PR, Pierre, of course it is, we both understand that, but PR can be very powerful. I wish it didn't have to be this way, but politics isn't how we thought it was going to be.

Pierre

She is a kid.

Howard

It doesn't matter who she is.

She could be a half-wit. Just so long as the people get behind her, see her as their own.

Pierre

She spoke French.

Howard

We will look after her.

Yes, alright, Kiki, you can go, but don't go far. I'll need you back here.

Kiki

Thank you.

Kiki goes.
Howard speaks to Pierre alone.

Howard

Is there something else going on with this woman?

Pierre

Of course not.

Howard

Then no arguments, we'll use her.

73

Pierre looks out of the window again.

What else do we know about her?

Pierre
Not much.

Howard
Where does she come from?

Pierre
I told you everything I knew. She left a card for the organisation. She had a caterpillar crawling up her shirt, and her hands when she put them on my forehead felt like melted butter.

Howard
What time were you expecting her?

Pierre
First thing – what time is it?

Howard
You do realise if she doesn't turn up, we have a problem. I mean, I know she will, I am just saying.

Pierre
My head starts to ache when you talk about problems.

Howard
I mean now we have promised the international community this thing, everyone is going to be very interested to see how it evolves.

Pierre
She will turn up.

Howard
It has gone twelve. That isn't first thing.

Pause.
They wait for a minute.

She knew where to come?

Pierre
She was here last night.

Howard
Of course she was.

Beat.

You do realise the stakes of this now?
We want these international businesses to come, we need to get our house in order. You just don't look on edge, quite enough, could you sit more restlessly, or pace about?

Howard's phone goes again.
He answers it.

Hello.
Yeah, I have got him here.
Yes, well can't you read it out. OK, send it up.

Pause.
Pierre looks at him.

I fucking hate the feeling. This feeling I am feeling right now. I fucking hate it.

Beat.
A woman comes in with a note.
Howard takes it, the woman leaves.

It is in French.
What is the point of that? Fucking French.

Pierre takes it.

You are really going to need to do your magic now, Pierre.

Pierre
She is sorry. She needs to go away.
Unexpectedly.

Pierre drops the note.

Howard
She is lying, of course.

Pierre
Of course she is.

Howard
She is smarter than she appeared, then.

Pierre
Maybe.

Howard picks it up.

Howard
Chicken.
Chicken cunt.
OK, so we lost a woman. How many fucking women are there in this country? We find another woman – you wave that magic wand of yours and make a woman appear. We need a woman, you understand.

Pierre
You said she was the woman.

Howard
But any woman will do.

Pierre
She held my head.

Howard
Oh bloody stop this, Pierre, please.
No wonder it gets on Kiki's nerves.

He picks up the phone.

Kiki, come back here.

Pierre

Kiki can't do it.

Howard

Of course she can't do it, I am not being bloody stupid, but she is a woman, isn't she, she knows where we will be able to get one from. What does this note actually say, can you translate it word for word for me.

Pierre

I need to go away. Unexpectedly.
    I can't do it.

Howard

These last words?

Pierre

Sorry.

Howard

In French.

Pierre

Avec regret.

Howard

Two in French, only one in ours?
    We are in a lot of shit, you know that.

Kiki comes in.

Kiki

What is going on?

Howard

We need a woman.

Kiki

OK.

Howard

Do you think you can arrange that?

Kiki

Probably, for this?

Howard

Just someone who has three spare days to give.
Someone educated, someone who can listen. Who
wants to learn, who can take responsibility, can make a
decision, isn't rash, is plausible.

Kiki

Should I be writing this down?

Howard

Actually she should be more than that. She should feel
like she is one of the people, she should represent
something for them before we even start. It could be a
blessing this, our first one was too young. And she
came from London – how were we going to cover that
up? You are right, we need someone else. Your
brilliance again. We need an icon. That is what we are
talking out.

Kiki, go out and find me an icon.

Kiki

An icon?

What do you mean? A pop star?

Howard

No.

Someone they already know. Someone already
connected to this whole thing. Someone who fascinates
them. Intrigues them. Someone whose face has been in
the papers already.

Silbermann's wife.

That is who we need.

She can bloody do it.

SCENE SIX

Justine is sitting on a bench.
Liddel appears with flowers and a green dress.

Liddel
Have you seen Kate?
Only I recognise you from the same hotel.

Justine
No, I haven't seen her.

Liddel
OK. I'll wait
How is your campaign going?

Justine
OK.

Liddel
I heard there has been a stay of execution, well done.
Thought that must have had something to do with you.

Justine
Not really.

Liddel
You're modest.
That is a very nice trait.
I expect you got a promotion. A bonus. I bet everyone is really pleased with you.

Beat.

Justine
I should go.

Liddel
If you see Kate, tell her I am waiting.

Justine

OK.

Liddel

I am hoping she is going to say yes to me today.
I have got a ring in my pocket.
What do you think? Do I look lucky?

Justine starts to walk away.

Justine

You haven't heard the news?

Liddel

No I've been driving. The radio in my car doesn't work.

Justine

Listen to the news.

Liddel

Is Kate OK?

Justine

You need to listen to the news.

Liddel

You are scaring me.

Beat.
She lets him listen to her portable radio with earphones.
When he has finished.

So they are going to kill her.

Justine

No.

Liddel

It will destroy her. Oh God. I knew she should have come home with me.

Justine

It won't destroy her.

Liddel

I am sorry, but I don't think you know what you are talking about.

Beat.

Justine

They needed a woman, that was all.

Liddel

Kate isn't a woman.

How can you say she is a woman? Don't you see, she is nothing but a child.

Liddel leaves the flowers and the dress.

SCENE SEVEN

Kate is in the box. Listening in the headphones. Kiki is sitting outside, talking to her.

Kiki

Just as well you have headphones on. I didn't mean exactly that. But you have to admit there is a lot of intrigue about you. I read an article, I would call you neither loved not loathed, but people, they want to know more. They think that women have intuition, I think that is it. Women are supposed to know about these things, to be able to spot things in a man, so when someone doesn't, we think, how can that be? She *must* have known who he was, however much she protests. Or that is what I think it is, anyway. Plus you have good bone structure, you take a good photo, that always helps.

Howard comes in.

Howard

You shouldn't be in here.

Kiki
Someone needs to sit with her.

Howard
There was an attendant.

Kiki
I sent him away.

Howard
How is she doing?

Kiki
She hasn't moved, so far.

Howard
Has she asked for water?

Kiki
No.

Howard
She can have water if she wants it. And a break every four hours.

Kiki
She doesn't want to break.

Howard
How do you know?

Kiki
That is what the attendant said. When it came to the last one she asked to carry on.

Howard
She looks smaller close up.

Kiki
Icons always do.

Howard looks at Kate.

Howard

She isn't blinking.

Kiki, she is white as a sheet. She should be taking a break.

When did she last drink?

Kiki

I didn't notice.

Did Pierre go on to you this morning about talking French again? I feel I am losing him, Howard.

I think maybe if I had a baby . . .

Howard looks at Kiki.

Howard

Are you joking? That is the last thing any of us need.

Kiki

Do you care about my marriage at all?

Howard

Not particularly. I wonder where she has got to, in the tape.

Kiki

Howard?

Howard

I know that the man who put the tapes together, well he, we had to change men halfway through, they . . . I think we should insist that she takes a break. She isn't blinking at all. Isn't that bad for your eyeballs if you do that?

He waves his hand in front of the glass.

Kiki

She can't see through the glass.

Howard

She might register the change in light, just enough to make her blink.

She is white as a sheet.
I'm going to stop the tape. Check she is OK. Do you think I should?

Kiki

She must know it all, anyway.

Howard

But what if she doesn't?
That is what she always claimed, maybe it was the truth.

He looks at her again.

I'm going in.

He opens the door to the glass booth.
Kate crashes to the floor.

Lock the doors, Kiki.
Oh fuck.

Kiki

What's wrong?

Howard

She isn't breathing, her pulse is all over the place.

He slaps her around the face.

Your heart can't stop beating just from listening to something, can it?

Kiki

I'll get Pierre.

Howard

Get some water, that is the first thing, we need to chuck some water in her face.

Kiki

The taps aren't working down here, it's the attendant who brings water.

Howard
Well go and get the attendant then.

Kiki
You told me to lock the doors.

Howard
Piss on her, then, I don't care, we have to wake her up.

Kiki comes over.

Kiki
There is a pressure point. Behind the neck. Press it.
Another on the feet.
Squeeze hard there, she has only passed out.

Howard
It looks like a coma.

Kiki
You overreact.

Kate starts to come round.

I told you the pressure point.
Kate?

Kate looks from one to the other.
She retches.

Get a bowl, she's going to be sick.

Howard
We locked the doors.

Kiki
Give me your fucking shoe, then.

Howard gives Kiki his shoe.
Kate pukes in it.

I need the other one.
What? You aren't going to wear them now, are you?

Howard gives her his other shoe.
Kate is sick in that one too.

Howard
Kate, talk to me. You need to have a break. This isn't supposed to be torture.

Kate shakes her head.

Kiki
We think you should stop for the day.

Howard
Even maybe totally, you have done enough.
You can make the decision now, if you want.

Kate speaks quietly.

Kiki
Say that again.

Kiki puts her ear up close to Kate so that she can hear.

She wants to go back in the box.

Howard
Have a break first.

Kate
No, no break.

She stands up, she is wobbly.
They steady her.
She takes a few steps.
Falls over.
They rush to her.

I am sorry, my legs don't seem to work.

She is sick again.

Howard
You can't go back in there.
It is too much in one go.

Kate

I will crawl back in there if I have to. I have to finish.
Don't help me stand. I can crawl.

She crawls back in.

Howard

We will have to ring the attendant, get the doors
unlocked.

Clear up all this.

Beat.

Kiki. This is between you and me. If she can't do it, we
will think of something else, this can't backfire. It's too
important now. Too big, I have got most of the world's
press watching, Malacont, Russia, the OHF. I'll sign for
her, show the press her signature, and be done with it.
We know that she will decide to execute them anyway –
no one can listen to all that and decide anything else.

Pierre comes in.

Pierre

I heard the doors being locked.

Howard

She isn't doing well.

Kiki

She puked all over the floor.

Pierre

What did you do?

Howard

We tried to give her water.

Kiki

We tried to make her stop.

Pierre

You can't do that, that isn't what she needs.

Howard

How do you know what she needs?

Pierre

It is what I have been trying to tell you both.
She needs someone to hold her head.

Kiki

This again.
Oh Howard, I can't stand it.

Pierre

Someone to sit with her.

Kiki

This is it, this is what I am talking about.

Howard

Don't do this now.

Kiki

But where did he get it from?

Pierre

I got it because I am still a person. Open the door, I'm
going in.

He tries to go in. Howard stops him.

Howard

We have to end it, this was an experiment that went
too far.

Pierre

What did you expect, she would sit there and breeze
through it, come out and thank us for the experience?

Howard

I have around a hundred press photographers sitting
outside this room. They are all waiting to take a
picture of her making a decision. If she collapses on us
before she decides, stops breathing –

Pierre

This is your circus, Howard, you handle it.

Pierre looks at Kate.

Kiki

Can just listening really kill someone? Could she die in there?

Pierre

I have no bloody idea.

Pierre goes in.
He turns the tape off.
He takes the headphones off her head.
He supports her as she walks out.

She needs a chair, for God's sake, Kiki.

Kiki gets a chair.
Howard produces a piece of paper.

Kate, can you hear me?
We are going to call an end to this.

Howard

We going to ask you to decide now.

Pierre

Don't be ridiculous.

Howard

Just give her the option.
She has heard more than half already, and that is enough.
Can you sign? Decide one way or another.

She says neither yes nor no.

Pierre

No one is forcing you.

She nods, a very slight movement, but it is there.

Kiki

She said yes.

Pierre

OK, Howard, bring them in.
Let's get it over and done with.

Howard opens the doors.
In come the press, with chaos and flashes and live
cameras.
For a second it is overwhelming.

Act Two

The prison cell.
Evener is very badly beaten. He is hardly recognisable
from the scene before.
Justine is with him.

Justine
There are some things that you are entitled to.
I realise this is a difficult time, and you may not
want to think about anything now. I have it all written
down on a piece of paper. I can leave it with you, if
you would prefer. Or read it out. The light in here
may not be that good for you – perhaps I should read
it out?

Beat.
Evener doesn't say anything.

Everyone wants to make you as comfortable as possible.
You have some rights to that. To dignity, if nothing
else. I can arrange for you to see a priest, or someone
else if you want.

Evener
My mother?

Justine
Yes, I am sure if you . . .

Evener
She is dead.
It was a joke.

Justine
Oh.

Evener

Do go on.

Justine

I can be with you, if you would like. Or someone from my organisation.

We can accompany you, right up to the last minute. You don't have to go through it alone.

Evener says nothing.

I'll leave a card.

I can come back later, if you would prefer that. We can talk more then.

Evener

I would like to see my mother, though. That is the strange thing. I haven't thought about her for years, but now . . .

I used to laugh at the soldiers when they cried out for their mums.

Ironically.

Justine

Of course you are scared.

Evener

Do you believe in Hell?

Beat.

Justine

No.

Evener

Then neither do I. My mum always said you should – you know, just in case.

Justine

Maybe I should get the priest.

Evener

No.

I'll stop.

I thought I saw her last night. In here with me. I thought I saw her face. Maybe she will be there on the other side, maybe the two of us will sit in Hell together, roast our toes.

Do you believe that as you get close to your death, the walls between the two get very thin? So thin you can stretch across and almost touch?

Justine

I don't have any religious beliefs.

Evener

You must believe something, we all believe something.

Justine

Not really.

Evener

My father, when I was a boy. He took me over to the fridge. Come here son, he said. See all this talk of the afterlife. It's a lie. He unplugged the fridge, ripping out the wires. Death, it's like that he said. One minute you're there and switched on, the next nothing.

Beat.
Justine doesn't know what to say.
Neither does Evener.

Justine

I got a tape. In case you needed some music.

Evener

Let me see.

Justine shows him.

Fucking opera.

Justine

I don't know how you are going to play it.

Why don't you ask for a tape machine, as your
official request?

Evener

I didn't ask for a tape. I hate fucking opera.
Maybe that is what I will find in Hell. Years and
years of opera.

Evener tries to move.
He is in pain.
He winces.

Justine

Do you want me to get someone to look at that?

Evener

Please tell me that was a joke.
I can't stand up.
They have broken both my legs, so God knows how
they think I am going to walk to the execution ground.
Tell me what you see out of the window.
That is my official request. You wanted it, here it is.
Describe the scene.

Justine

Plums.

Evener

I know about the plums. They are past their best
though, now. Even the wasps have stopped coming.

She walks over to have a better look.

Justine

I can see . . .

She looks out of the window.

I can see the square.

Evener
I imagined that you would.

Justine
The houses.

Evener
I know about the houses.

Justine
There is nothing else, really.

Evener
Credit me with something.

Beat.

Justine
The sun is setting. It is difficult for me to see.

Evener
My legs don't work. You didn't tell me your name, so I don't know how to address you.

Justine
Justine.

Evener
Justine, they have broken both my legs so my chance of looking out of the window is several thousand to one.

Justine
There are children playing.

Evener
I am not interested in children.

Beat.

Tell me about the man with the plank of wood. And his friends beside him. Tell me how easily these planks are going into the ground, and the shape of the construction that they make.

Tell me if they are joking. Is there one of them that is cracking jokes to make it easier for all of them, or are they all in a good mood? Is the ground soft?

Tell me.

Beat.

Or if you won't tell me, then fuck off. But don't kid yourself that you are helping people like me.

Justine
The construction is nearly finished.

Evener
Thank you.

Justine
They're putting the last few pieces of wood in place.

Evener
I keep hearing clanks.

Justine
It is nearly done.

Evener
There are so many clanks.

Like there is more wood arriving. I heard a van before, and could hear another pile being unloaded. If they are finished, why are they bringing more wood from the van?

Justine
There is a second construction.

Evener
Ah.

A second construction?

Justine
There is a small crowd.

Evener

Small?

Justine

Large.

The second construction is for the crowd.

Beat.

Evener

I have heard in America you die in your own box with only your family looking on. You know what I keep thinking about, and I know this will sound crazy, but what happens if I don't die? They have got their measurements wrong – or me, perhaps it is this old body after all that defies nature, and Rasputin-like it fails to break.

Justine

I don't think it is likely.

Evener

But imagine.

I swing, and smile.

The crowd gasps.

How can it be, they say to each other. They put their hands over their children's eyes.

That man should be dead.

Someone swings on my legs, blaming the executioner.

They cut me down, try a bullet in my head, but even the bullet bounces, ricocheting off the buildings behind. They try a knife, the skin won't break. I am totally indestructible. Imagine that.

Beat.

It's a good joke. I always loved a good joke.

Justine

I'll leave these for you.

And if you want a priest, if you change your mind –

Evener

They'll shoot us, won't they? Not hang us.

Justine

I don't know.

Evener

I would if I were them. Let the blood flow. Give the crowd some drama. What is the matter, are you finding this too upsetting? Too direct? You want to go now?

Beat.

What if I did ask you to accompany me?

Justine

That is what we are here for.

Evener

Walk down the steps with me, see the whole thing through.

Justine

It's part of my job.

Evener

Go home, Justine.

Drink.

Sleep. Forget about me.

Justine

If you asked it, I would be there.

Evener

There is a rumour inside here, I heard that there are stalls out there selling souvenirs.

Beat.

Justine
I'll leave the card.

SCENE TWO

Kiki and Howard meet in a corridor.

Howard
Steer him away, for God's sake, Kiki.

Kiki
I do, I try to, it's difficult.

Howard
Create some domestic crisis or something.

Kiki
I can't stop him asking about it.

Howard
Of course you can.

Kiki
It's a valid question.

Howard
He shouldn't even be thinking about that woman, he should be thinking about what comes next.

Kiki
With all the publicity?

Howard
That will calm down soon.

Kiki
Her face is on every magazine, every page of the newspaper.

Howard

I didn't anticipate quite this reaction.

Kiki

It's like she is a national saviour.

Howard

We just have to get through the next couple of days.

Kiki

She has gone from the most hated, to the most loved.
They are ravenous for her, the more they can get.

Howard

I accept it's a bit tricky.

Kiki

Tricky?

Howard

That it might feel out of control.

Kiki

It will occur to someone else soon.
Pierre will ask it publicly, or start asking his other advisers, and they will ask each other and then their wives, and before you know where you –

Howard

That is why we have to keep all these articles up, all these interviews.

Kiki

We can't do it.

Howard

We have one more day, Kiki.
Get it under control, one more day. Then they are executed.
We can do anything.

Kiki

I have written twenty interviews this evening as it is,
all pretending to be Kate Griselle.

Howard

So do forty.

Kiki

It is total madness. And dangerous. This isn't a game.
I can't take on someone else's identity.

Howard

Others do.

Kiki

Someone will work it out. Someone will think it's a bit
odd that there are no new photos to go with all these
articles. Someone else will ask when did anyone last
see her?

Howard

One day.

Kiki

I hate it, that is all I am saying. It scares me, and puts
me on edge –

Howard

I know.

Kiki

I'm not a politician, I didn't sign up for this.
And I hate lying to Pierre.
That especially.

Howard

Oh come on.

Kiki

I do.

Howard

It's not like you haven't done that before.

Kiki

Why did you say that?

Beat.

Howard

I'm grateful for everything that you are doing, I realise you don't have to.

Kiki

I would rather you didn't put your hand on me.

Howard

Keep your nerve, that is what I mean.
Particularly with Pierre.

Kiki

Take your hand off me.

Howard

It's important, Keeks. I don't need to spell out how important, do I?
I need to be able to rely on you.
You and me, we are the team.

Beat.

You understand?

Kiki

Yes.

He is still holding her arm.
He lets go.

Howard

You are a good friend. The best.

Kiki

What was that?

Howard
    That was nothing, Kiki.

Beat.

That was friendship, loyalty. Get a grip, do what you
    have to do.

SCENE THREE

Pierre and Kiki are in their bedroom, getting undressed.

Pierre
    You OK?

Kiki
    Yes, you?

Pierre
    Fine.

Beat.

Do you want to lie down, or just go straight to sleep?
    Hold each other or something?

Kiki
    OK.

Pierre
    Or is there no point?

Kiki
    What do you mean, no point?

Pierre shrugs.

You want me to hold your head, speak French, is that it?

Pierre
    No.

Kiki

I don't speak French particularly, but I suppose I could learn. Get better. If you wanted me to, if it really was so important to you.

Pierre

Not really.

Beat.
Kiki gets into bed.

Kiki

Sometimes I wish I had the energy I had at the start.

Pierre

I'm tired, I have had a long day.

He sits on the bed too.
She puts her hand out to him.
He takes it.
He sort of slumps, loses all his resistance.
Might cry.

Kiki

Don't do that.
Please don't do that.

Pierre

Mistakes.
Mistakes I have made. Am making.
And your hand.
Which I am trying to despise.

Kiki

What?

Pierre

Please don't ask me why.

Beat.
He holds on to her hand tightly.

I am trying so hard to despise but all I can get is indifference.

Kiki

Pierre, look at me.

Pierre

If I wasn't so exhausted I could spend hours trying to work out what it is, why you won't look me in the eye any more. Why you and me sleep on different shifts, why we don't talk, we don't even bicker. And Howard is the same. If I wanted I could think about it, stew on it, what you and Howard might be talking about, whispering about, how come it is that everyone else knows more about everything than me, what the big fucking secret is, but you know the saddest thing of all? I really don't care.

Kiki

Don't do this.

Pierre

Where is she?
I have asked you before, I have asked him.
I feel like I am whispering now, hardly heard.
Where is she?
Where is she? All day long.

Beat.

I'm getting into bed. I'm going to turn the light out and go to sleep.
Forget I spoke.
Whatever it is, it is bigger than me.
You either know something or you don't. Either way we are screwed.

He gets into bed.

It must be possible to learn to hate you. In time.

Kiki

Please don't say that.

Pierre

You cried the other day and I felt it still, but as
I watched you I was thinking, what is this? It's only
a feeling. You can train yourself out of a feeling.

Of course the marriage is a sham – everything else
is, so why am I surprised that we are here too?

Pierre sits up and looks at Kiki.
Kiki is motionless, she doesn't know what to do.

He killed her.

Kiki

No.

Pierre

She has gone insane, she is sick.

Kiki

Nothing like that.

Pierre

Then what?

Beat.

Kiki

Don't make me.

Pierre

Oh fuck it, Kiki, I don't know.

Of course I won't make you, I never do. That is our
problem.

Forget it. Forget it all.

Beat.

Kiki

She changed her mind.

Beat.

She changed her mind.

Pierre
Kiki, tell me you are joking.

Kiki
No.
It was after she signed, and we all saw her sign, the next day, before she was due to go home, she asked for a bath. Please listen to me, Pierre, I never meant to get involved in this –
Some water, she said, I helped her run it. And I watched her wash herself.
She was still shaking after the ordeal, and was so white.
She asked for a towel.
Then very quietly told me, she had made a mistake.
She thought perhaps she had made a mistake.

Beat.

How could I tell you?

Pierre
I don't know, Kiki, you tell me.

Kiki
Are you fucking stupid?
It was all over the papers by then.

Pierre
Tomorrow we are executing fourteen men because she said so, and she changed her mind?

Kiki
I told Howard.

Pierre
I can't believe this.

Kiki

I know I made a mistake, I should have come straight to you – that is why I am telling you now.

Pierre

Now? You are telling me now?

Kiki

I said I am sorry.

Pierre

So what, you have her hidden? Imprisoned? What?

Pierre comes round and grabs her.

Where the hell is she?

Kiki

Just resign, leave this, leave this to Howard, you've been wanting to.

Pierre

How can you have any loyalty left to him?

Kiki

This isn't your game, this isn't what you are good at –

Pierre

Tell me where she is.

Kiki

It's settled now. Everything is settled. The executions are tomorrow.

Pierre

Her face is on the fucking T-shirts, Kiki. This is the only thing she will be remembered for, and if she had even the slightest doubt. For a second . . .

Kiki

He convinced me it was the right thing to do, I don't know why I agreed, he manipulates me too, he gets in my mind.

Pierre
　The exact address.

Kiki
　I don't have it any more.

Pierre
　Kiki.

He slaps her.
She sits upright.

Kiki
　I can't say any more, I've said enough.
　　Leave the rest to the real politicians.

Pierre
　I'll slap you again.

Kiki
　I just want you to be the old Pierre. As it used to be.
　　You slap me again, I'll slap you.

Pierre
　Fine.

He slaps her.
She slaps him back.
They wrestle.

　You have no idea how important this is.

Kiki
　Of course I do.

They wrestle some more.

Pierre
　Oh, fuck you.

He drops her and walks away.
Kiki sits by herself on the bed.

Kiki

You are going to screw everything. You go after her, you don't know what you are doing.

Pierre

Everything is screwed anyway.

Kiki

Not true, Howard says the investment is just –

Pierre

Howard again?

Beat.

Me or Howard, Kiki?

Beat.

Kiki

She is in Swan Valley. A tiny settlement called Korona. There are only three houses, the others are empty.

Pierre

What was the plan?

Kiki

There wasn't a plan.

Pierre

For afterwards?
What was going to happen to her afterwards?

Kiki shrugs.

Kiki

No one was thinking that far ahead.

Pierre puts his clothes back on.
He carries on getting dressed.

I can grow up, I can change.

Pierre

Forget it, Kiki.

He goes out.

SCENE FOUR

A little cottage. A little kitchen.

Kate and Liddel.
Beat.

Kate

I am not interested in the moon.

Liddel

It's very bright, that's all, surprisingly bright.

You could sit on the step, I am sure they wouldn't mind if you sat on the step. I could open the door, we could drink something. Listen to some music.

We are getting married someday, after all.

Kate goes and gets the old tin tub.

What are you doing?

Kate

I feel dirty.

Liddel

There is very little water, I told you, what there is is cold.

Kate

Then I will wash in very little.

Kate starts taking her clothes off.

Liddel

Kate, stand back from the window, they will see you.

Kate

I don't care if they see me.

What, this haggard old body? They might as well get a good look.

Liddel

I wish there were curtains.

Kate

Let them look.

Liddel

I'll turn the light off, then.

Kate

I am simply taking a bath. If they are to imprison me, then they can watch me wash. I am not going to have a bath in the dark at my age, just because I am worried that they might see.

Liddel tries to cover her.
He takes the tablecloth off the table and tries to hang it against the window.

Beat.

There is a river, anyway.

If you prefer we could steal down to the river. Wash in as much water as you could ask for?

Liddel

You know we can't do that.

Kate

It's dark, they won't even see.

Liddel

They would catch us.

Kate

They catch us, they bring us back here.

What are they going to do?

Liddel

Break our backs.

Beat.

Kate

Why did you say that?
 Why on earth did you say that?

Beat.

Liddel

I don't know.

Kate

Tell me why you said that?

Liddel

You say it.
 I said it because you say it.
 You say it all the time in your sleep.

Beat.

Kate

Do I?

Liddel

Yes.
 And more.

Beat.
Kate puts both taps on full.

That is enough water.

Kate

It is hardly covering my ankles.
 It is just water, Liddel, what do you think I am
 going to do, make ropes out of it and string them
 around my neck. You are here, with me. I am taking
 a bath.

Liddel

I am worried about you, Kate. That is all.

There is no point getting married if I can't love you.

Kate says nothing.

I saw another ring today.

In a shop when I went to town. I nearly bought it.

Kate

Is it pretty?

Liddel

It's plain, like you.

But the most beautiful thing I ever saw.

Kate

Will you scrub my back?

Liddel

Of course.

She turns the taps off.

Kate

Please don't quote anything I say in my sleep back to me.

Liddel

I didn't mean to.

Kate

Leave it in the realm of sleep.

What sleep there is. It is not as if I do sleep. Or haven't now for days. I get nervous as the days wear on knowing that there will come a point when you will say that you are tired, because you will need to sleep even if I don't. And you can't help it, but you leave me. Every night you go off and you leave me.

Liddel

I am right beside you.

Kate

But you are somewhere that I can never be ever again.
I long to sleep like you, Liddel. You don't know
how much you can long for sleep and never get there.

Liddel

I do.

Kate

No, you see a tired woman and you think, poor
exhausted Kate.

I am trapped, Liddel. I am back in that box. But this
box I made myself. You know why I want to bathe all
the time? Just because while I am in this water, this
freezing cold water, I can feel a little of what it used to
be like to be living.

Liddel

It's tomorrow.

Beat.

I bought a newspaper.
Tomorrow morning, first thing.
There is a public holiday.

Beat.

At least it will be over.
This time tomorrow, it will be over.

Kate says nothing.

Won't it?

Kate

For them, yes.

He washes her.

You are a doctor. You tell me, what happens to people
if they don't sleep?

Liddel

Everyone sleeps in the end.

Kate

Not me.

Liddel

So you will sleep soon.

Kate

I'll never sleep again. I know I won't.

Liddel

I will get you some tablets next time they let me go into town.

Kate

You got me some.

Liddel

Stronger.

Kate

How strong would they have to be?
Nothing has made me sleep so far.

Liddel

The images will go away soon.

Kate

It isn't the images of what they did that haunt me.
Oh yes, they are bad, but –
It's me.
It's what I did.
I heard on the radio. There is a radio upstairs, you have not cleared this place as effectively as you thought. There is a radio upstairs, and I heard my name. Kate Griselle. I tried to change the channel but my name was on the other side. I keep turning the knob, but I couldn't escape it. Even in foreign languages my name was there. This name that is mine, Kate Griselle.

Liddel

I will help you if I can, Kate.
You know I will do whatever you want.
I'll stay awake with you.

Kate

You'll try.
For the first night, but for the second?
Anyway, what good does your insomnia do mine?

Liddel

You were set up to fail, you know that.

Kate

When I was young I read about a girl in some story,
you will probably know it.

Liddel

Which story?

Kate

It doesn't matter, she was dead and in the underworld.
But they took her down to the river and bathed her,
as soon as she was in the water she forgot everything
about her life. The whole lot was wiped.

Liddel sits on the end of the bath.

Wash me.

Beat.

Get in the bath and wash me.

Liddel

Kate?

Kate

What? We are both adults. We are going to be married.

Liddel

What if the guards see?

Kate
    What if they do?

Liddel looks at the window. Then takes his clothes off.
He gets into the bath.

Liddel
    Ahh.

Kate
    Freezing.

Liddel
    Yes.

Kate
    I won't make you take a cold bath with me again.

Liddel
    No?

Kate
    No.

He gets fully in.

    I can't live this life.
        You know that, don't you?
        I know you must know it because you have
    removed everything sharp from the kitchen.

Liddel
    Kate, please.

Kate
    So we have a choice. Either we live here for a few
    more weeks, with you watching my every move,
    locking everything up, and us both waiting for the
    time when you slip up, you leave something out, a
    shoelace or a piece of glass that I can break. Something
    that I can find that I can use, and I am resourceful, you
    know I am, wily and manipulative.

Liddel
You will get better.

Kate
I cannot get better from this. Because it is a condition of
my own making.

Liddel
Please don't talk like this.

Kate
Hold my head under the water.

Beat.

You can't drown yourself, I heard a programme about
it once. It isn't possible.

Liddel
This is madness.

Kate
I am begging you with everything I have.

Beat.
He reaches forward and kisses her.
He gets out of the bath.

So you don't love me.

Liddel
I love you more than life itself.

Kate
I will do it without you.

He takes a towel. Starts to dry himself.
Someone knocks at the door.

Don't answer it.

They knock again.

I'll smash a window. Cut myself to smithereens. Wipe myself all over the walls. I will make the most incredible mess. You will have to wipe me from the floor.

Liddel
I have to answer it.

Kate
If you answer it, it will be the guards and they will have heard us and they will take me away from you, and then I will never be able to escape.

I need you to do this for me.

More knocks at the door.
He starts to cry.

Liddel
All I ever did was love you.

Kate
Give me your hand.

Liddel
I can't do it, Kate.

The knocking becomes more insistent.

Kate
Quickly, please.

Liddel
I can't.

Kate
Then let me do it for you. Please, Liddel, all I am asking for is to be let go. You know I won't get better, we will never marry. If you don't do it, I will. And then I will be properly alone.

He gives her his hand.
She puts it on her head.

Keep it firm.
>I might struggle, but keep it firm.
>I have written a note. It explains it all.
>No one will blame you.

She goes under the water, with his hand.

Liddel
>Wait.
>>Another second.
>>Please.
>>Another second with me.

Kate stops. She puts her face over to his. They kiss.
Fondly. A goodbye.
The person on the other side of the door is keen to get in,
starts to call.

Kate
>Quickly now.

Liddel
>Are you sure you want this?

Kate
>I am trapped.
>>A caged animal in a box.

She goes under the water, with his hand.
He holds it there.
And holds it there.
Kate struggles, her legs kick.
He keeps holding it there.
A full minute passes. It seems to go on for ages.
Finally she is still.
He howls out in pain.
He lifts her dead body out of the bath.
She is limp.
He cradles her and cries.
He holds her for a minute. He wipes her head.

He kisses her.
He cries again.
He doesn't move.
He wraps her in a towel.
He goes to the door and unlocks it.
Pierre comes in, sees the situation.
Liddel speaks quietly.

Liddel
Arrest me. Please.
You must have seen it all through the window. Take me away now.

Pierre
Oh my God.

Pierre grabs Kate's body and tries to revive her.

Liddel
She's dead.

Pierre
We might get her back.
I came for her.

Liddel
Too late.

He pushes Pierre.
He reaches for some keys in his pocket.

There are knives in this house, I know there are because I locked them up, but now I am going to get them to cut right through you.

Pierre
Please let me help her.

Liddel
She is dead, I told you.

Liddel drops the keys he was fumbling with.

He howls and crumbles to the floor.
Pierre tries to catch him.

Pierre

I didn't hear until today. Seven hours ago, I heard about Kate.

I have been driving through the night to get here.

I have been asking my advisers, what happened to her?

Beat.

Please listen to me.

I didn't know this happened, the police guard, her realisation.

I didn't realise she changed her mind.

Liddel

You drove her insane.

Pierre

But she wasn't insane, no. She was clear thinking and free.

Please listen to me, her mind was clearer than anybody else's. She was able to think one thing and later to think another.

I'm going to cancel tomorrow.

Beat.

No one will be shot tomorrow, not in her name.

Get the knife that you talked about, hold it up to my neck and make sure I do it.

Beat.

Liddel

She was an extraordinary woman.

Pierre

I am beginning to understand that.

Liddel
I promised her I wouldn't leave her.

Pierre
We can bury her outside.

Liddel
The ground is hard as iron.

Beat.

Go without me, I want to stay with her.

Pierre
No, you have to come.
This is her finest hour, celebrate it with her.

Beat.

Liddel
I can't leave her here.

Pierre
She has gone. Listen to me.
She has gone.
It's her legacy that is important now.

Pierre hands Liddel the knife.

Take the knife.
Keep it at my back.

SCENE FIVE

The prison cell.
A guard is sweeping it out. Picking up pieces of rubbish and putting them in a black bag.
Justine comes in.

Guard
Gone.

Justine
Oh.

Guard
Hours ago. They carried him down.

Justine
I said I would be here if he wanted . . .

Guard
You missed it.

Justine
Can't I . . . ?

Guard
Nope. Not now.
You can watch from here, if you want. Next best thing.

Justine
I said I would help him.

Guard
I don't suppose he will hold it against you.

He whistles as he works. Justine looks at him uneasily. He comes quite close to her.

Justine
I think I should go back out.

Guard
You won't get back out now.
They will have locked the doors.
Special rules on special days.
You are stuck in here now, until it is over.

Justine
How long?

The Guard looks at his watch.

Guard
'Bout an hour and a half.

He whistles again.

I've got an erection.
Just in case you are interested.

Beat.

In the old days when someone was being shot, almost every day I used to be stiff the whole time. It's not just me, you ask just about anyone that works here.
Sex and death.
It's exciting.
Don't tell me you aren't wet.

He whistles the tune again.

Ninety minutes to go.

Justine
Don't touch me.

Guard
It's just normal.
Anyway, like I said, I was just telling you. Letting you know.
Execution day. Seven a.m. They go from here.
That is when you should have been here. Should have asked me, I would have told you. Seven a.m. sharp.
Seven-oh-five they arrive downstairs. One set of keys does the first door.
Second set the second.
Three men, one on each side. The other behind. If they refuse to walk, *pssd*. With the electric ruler.
If they stumble.
Wham with the boot.
They walk.
Even your friend here will find he ends up walking.

They arrive in the preparation cell.

First they get seen by a priest. If they want. It's now about seven-fifteen. If they don't want a priest it's too bad. It just speeds the whole thing up, so they always see the priest.

They kneel. The innocent ones weep. The guilty howl.

The priest does all that shit. Last rites if they want it, or just a prayer. Now the priest has got an erection ten to one. Every man in the building is feeling excited in some way. It isn't just me, I told you, it's normal. Only they are wearing a cassock instead of these tight trousers so you can't see it.

Seven-thirty the priest goes out.

We get them to strip. Oh, they are the one that hasn't got a stiffy. Should have said that before, not every man. We get them to stand in a shower. There's a little shower in the corner of the room. Don't know why.

We wash them down.

The same guy always does it. Mushroom-head he is, huge great hands. He's gentle, no point being rough, just about to get it, aren't they.

Then we dress them.

New clothes. Usually the clothes they came in with if we still have them and they fit. They are clean, though, not like what they have been wearing in here. And pressed down. Collars starched. They have to go out those doors looking like the person the crowd wants to see. Recognise. No one wants to execute a down-and-out.

That is why they get a shower, I guess. Why they get a shave.

Seven-fifty the prison governer comes down.

Shakes them by the hand.

Runs though some procedural stuff. Tells them what is going to happen.

If they are going to pass out, it happens then.

That is why we have the three, and the one behind is nicknamed the catcher.

If they pass out it slows the whole thing down, to tell you the truth. Pain in the arse, and it can set you back by an hour.

Eight o'clock. Prison doctor comes. Takes the pulse. You can't execute someone who isn't healthy. Paradox, see. They have to have a health check.

Heart, lungs, eyes, tongue.

By then the main doors are opened and you can usually hear the crowd outside. Inside they start to do this thing with their eyes, all of them looking frantically from face to face.

Some of them sweat. Some call out to friends or lovers. Some shout. Some whisper. It's quite interesting how it takes people different ways.

The last thirty minutes are the worst. They sit on chairs, and wait. No one says much. Then, if there is a crowd, they come out for a parade.

You want to come to the window when it starts, you won't get a good view from there. What is the point in being here if you aren't going to watch?

Justine tries to get out.

What are you doing?

You are going the wrong way.

Justine

You have locked the door.

Guard

Of course I have.

I want you to watch it.

And I want you to watch it with me. It's the best thrill you get around here.

He grabs her by the hair.

She screams.
He puts his arms around her.

Watch it with me, you'll love it. I know you will. It's normal to love it.

He starts thrusting into her back.

We are going to watch from the window as they put the black bag over his head.

He is getting excited.

We are going to stand here and we see them shake in their boots.
And once they put the black bag over their heads, oh, now that is a good bit, you just fucking wait for that bit, ohh.
They get them to stand in a line.
Ohhh.
And they take aim.
And.
Bang.
Bang bang bang.
Fucking bang.

He comes all over her back.
They are both still for a second.
They he hits her, hard.

You fucking cunt.

He hits her again.

You fucking cunt. You made me come, they haven't even started yet.

He hits her again.

SCENE SIX

Howard and Kiki.

Howard

Where the fucking hell have you been?

Kiki

I've had a sore head.

Howard

Where is Pierre?

Kiki

He isn't back yet?

Howard

Back from where?

Kiki

I . . .

I don't know, he went out last night.

Howard

Kiki, look out of the window, there is a crowd of two hundred thousand outside. The ceremony was supposed to start an hour ago.

This isn't some normal Sunday morning.

Kiki

I know it isn't.

Howard

Everyone is waiting for Pierre to give the public signal.

I've been going out of my mind.

Kiki

I don't know where he is.

Howard

Well, bloody find him. It's you and me now, we have got to find him.

You don't mess with a crowd of two hundred thousand, not when they have been promised justice. I can hold off the start for another twenty minutes, but after that we will have to go ahead, Pierre or no Pierre.

Pierre comes in.

Thank God. Hurry.

Liddel is behind him.

We don't have time for where you have been or what you have been up to. The crowd are going crazy – have you heard what they are chanting?

Pierre
We have to cancel the executions.

Howard
What?

Pierre
Tell them what their hero really decided.
I'll go out the front, I will handle it.

Howard
What, while they are ripping your throat out?

Pierre
Kate was right.

Howard
It's immaterial.

Pierre
I have always been a pretty shit Prime Minister, I know that. You ran this place, whatever you say about magic, I never had a vision.

Howard
There is no time for this.

Pierre

But today for the first time I can see a way forward. A way that we don't have to go back into more killing and more conflict.

Howard

They will tear you to pieces.

Pierre

We shouldn't kill these men, that is what I will tell the crowd, we should pity them for what they became, we should wring our hands and lament where we went wrong to produce such ill specimens of humanity, and we should vow that this is a place where we should never again go.

That is the point.

We never go there again.

Howard

No one will listen.

Pierre

They have to listen. If one woman can find compassion after all that she heard, then we as a nation, as leaders of a nation –

There is an almighty crash. The window breaks.
Kiki goes to the window.

Howard

What the hell –

Kiki

It came from the crowd, someone threw something.

Pierre

Where are the police?

Howard

The police are there, but they haven't got riot gear.

Liddel

They are pushed right up against the gate.

Kiki

Christ, Pierre, you should see what they are carrying.

Howard

Start the fanfare. The ceremony. Pierre, give the order.
I've got a gun for you to fire the first shot.

Pierre

Please arrange for me to speak from a balcony.

Howard

You cannot do this –

Another crash.

Pierre

I can't not to do it.

Howard

You are out of your mind.

Pierre

We have turned them into bloodhounds, this isn't
justice.

Howard

You are risking everything, the whole country,
everything we have been working our bollocks off for
years, on this new folly. There are millions of men and
women and children out there who are relying on us to
get this right, to get this country back on its feet, and
we are here. We are bloody here.

Pierre

We are nowhere.

Howard

They are mass murderers.
That is what we are talking about here.

Pierre

No, we are talking about ourselves.

That is who we can save. There will always be the wicked, we can only save ourselves.

Howard

By letting monsters go free?

Pierre

No, not free, I never said free.

Just not shot like dogs.

It has got to be worth a try, maybe by some grace of God they see.

Kiki

There is a baby.

Pierre

What baby?

Kiki

Inside me.

Pierre

What is she talking about?

Kiki

Put your hand here, you'll feel.

So you can't die, you see? You can't go out there.

Pierre

A baby doesn't change anything. There are millions of babies out there.

Something else is thrown through the window. Outside a chant starts up.
Howard opens his bag.
He takes out a gun.

Kiki

Oh shit, no.

Howard –

Howard prepares it.

Howard
I will retire you off, if you like. Take you now under a guard and let you lie low. You and Kiki can go and have your baby.

Pierre
I will become the worst thorn in your side.

Howard
You will be out of the way.

Pierre
Everyone I meet I will tell about your deception and lies.

About the possibility we had, the rumours will spread.

If you cut out my tongue I would grow a new one.

Howard
They have to be executed.

Pierre kneels down in front of him.

Pierre
Then let the killing start here.

This is the nation's soul we are fighting for.

Is it to be death? Or something different?

Howard
What, though? You haven't told me what it will be.

Pierre
Because I don't know. Because it will be something complicated, something that will require us to be compassionate, to look at ourselves, to acknowledge difficult things.

It's easier to describe a hell than a heaven, a pain than an absence of one. We have fourteen words in our language for cruelty, but only one for hope.

Howard takes the gun.

Howard
You should have been a poet.
Not a politician.

Kiki
Oh God no.

Pierre
Isn't how a nation thinks more important than anything else?

Howard
Tell that to the slums.

Liddel
I have a knife, I won't let him hurt you.

Pierre
Hold on to it, old man.
Use it to fight him after I have gone.

Kiki
Howard –

Howard
Stop shouting, Kiki.

Another crash.

They are inside the courtyard.

Pierre
You know, Howard, I would rather be me at this instant than you, with all your impossibility of thought.

Kiki
NO.
Please, NO.

Howard shoots.

Pierre falls down dead.
Kiki rushes at the body.
Howard stands back, still with the gun.

Howard
Guard, tell the musicians, start up the fanfares.
  Quickly, and get the condemned out there.
  The crowd will get what they came for.
  He lost it – you understand that, Kiki.
  He was out of his mind. He couldn't see any more.

Howard looks at Liddel.

And you, old man, are you here to say the same
things?
  Pick up the knife and fight me?

Liddel
  I . . .

Beat.

Howard
  I am sorry, I didn't hear you.

Liddel
  No, I am just one of the crowd.
    I wandered this way.

Howard nods.

Howard
  Well, make sure you wander back.

Liddel hangs his head.
The fanfare starts.

Keeks?

She spits at him.

We will rebuild this place.
  I will rebuild this place.

Howard walks off.
Kiki and Liddel are left.
Liddel takes off his coat and puts it around her.
The drum rolls in the background.

Kiki

It's like I have been asleep for years, what has
happened.

I need to start to open my eyes.

The drum roll has stopped.

Why is that, why now silence?

They listen.

No sound even from the crowd, what is happening?

A shot is fired.
Then another. Then another.
There is a cheer.
Then more shots.

SCENE SEVEN

The shots continue.
Justine has found a small place away from the crowd.
She is frantic and scared, and trying to talk into her
mobile.

Justine

I need to talk to him. Quickly. He has to get me a
transfer – yes, I understand he is busy, but please take
a message. I have to get back to London. Today, today
if possible. Please organise someone in the office . . .

I am out here on my own.

Listen, I don't mean to be rude, but please fucking
get someone to get me out of here.

There is a shot in the background.

Yes, I heard it too. It is louder here
    I don't know if I am safe, that is the truth. That is
    why I am ringing.

Another shot.

   I'm going to get a taxi to the airport, if I can. There
   are so many people. I . . . I will ring you from the
   airport . . .
      The first flight. Whatever the cost. You understand?
      I don't care if you take it out of my wages or if I end
   up selling my flat to pay you back. I have to get out of
   here, immediately. I . . .
      Yes. Yes.
      Today. Please. Do what you can.

She puts the phone down.
The guard steps into her line of view.

Guard
   I acted like a fucking idiot back then. I don't know
   what came over me. I . . .
      Forgive me?

She walks away.
He shouts after her.

   Your loss.
      Your loss, baby.

SCENE EIGHT

In the mountains.
Liddel and Kiki are travelling by foot.

Kiki
   How much further?

Liddel

It is difficult to tell, normally when I do this route I drive.

Kiki

I don't think I can walk much more.

Liddel

We need a horse or a cart or something. I should pull you.

Pregnant women shouldn't have to walk.

Kiki

I didn't mind it at first.

But now I feel sick.

My back aches.

Liddel

Wait until later.

You think your back is aching now.

Beat.

I used to be a doctor.

Kiki

Oh.

Liddel

When we get there, you'll love the view, and the house. The house is the right place for a baby. Just let me see the map. There is a shading ahead, that might mean shelter.

Kiki

Can we sit down?

Liddel

It's getting dark.

Kiki

I can't walk much further.

Liddel

I think we should get to the shading.

Kiki

And if my back breaks?

Liddel

OK.

Kiki

I am not even wearing the right shoes for this, look at that.

He laughs.

Next time, I am not the woman to go on the run with.

Liddel

Take your shoes off.
You would be better going barefoot.

She takes them off.

Better.

Kiki

Yep.
But my feet will freeze.
It feels like winter already.

Liddel

It's still autumn.
We have a few weeks left. They won't freeze.

He lays down his coat for her.

There was a tree back there, we can sleep under it.
Tomorrow, we'll have to walk again. Further than today.

Kiki

It will get very dark here, won't it?
Away from the lights.

Liddel
Yep.

Kiki
In the city I was never really in the dark.

Liddel
We don't have electricity up in the mountains.

Kiki
You don't?

Liddel
No, you get used to the dark. Particularly in winter.
We have candles.

Liddel feels in his pocket.

I have some matches here.

He lights one.

Kiki
I don't like the dark. I don't like not being able to see.

Liddel
You get used to it.

Kiki
How many have you got?

Liddel
Enough.

He looks in the box.

Three.

Kiki
Don't waste them. Let's use them when it is really
dark.

Beat.

Liddel

There won't be electricity in the city soon.

When the oil runs out. The government will lose in the end. There'll be strikes, and power cuts, and less and less.

Even the people in the city will have to get used to the dark.

Kiki

And you tell me I should be happy.

About the baby.

Happy that I am bringing a baby into this? A baby, I don't even want a baby.

Liddel

You must want a baby.

Kiki

Why? Look at the world they inherit.

Liddel

Maybe the baby will sort it out.

Maybe it is this baby that will work out the answers.

Work out where we go from here.

Kiki

My baby?

Liddel

Why not?

Kiki

Or maybe this baby will just sit with us in the dark, and be scared.

Beat.

Liddel

Maybe.

Beat.

When is it due?

Kiki
In the spring.

Liddel
Then let's wait until the spring.
See who we get.

Kiki
We?

Liddel
I am not leaving you. Not now.
It is you, me and the baby now.

Kiki
And this world of nothing.
How long is it before the sun has fully gone down,
do you think?

Liddel
A few minutes.

Beat.

We still have a few matches left, remember.

Kiki
Yes, we still have a few matches.

The sun goes down.
The stage is in darkness.